BOOKS BY DENIS J. HAUPTLY

Journey From the Past
In Vietnam
"A Convention of Delegates"

" A CONVENTION OF DELEGATES"

The Creation of the Constitution

Frontis

*A drawing of an election day crowd in Philadelphia near the
Convention site in the late 1700s.*

"A Convention of Delegates"

The Creation of the Constitution

by

Denis J. Hauptly

STANDARD FEDERAL...
POUND RIDGE...
10576

ATHENEUM   New York   1987

J
342
H

50977

PICTURE CREDITS

Title page, 9, 25, 32-33, 36, 43, 79, 93—National Parks Service,
Department of the Interior
57—William Paterson College
70—Yale University Art Gallery
91—New-York Historical Society

Copyright © 1987 by Denis J. Hauptly

All rights reserved. No part of this book may be reproduced or transmitted
in any form or by any means, electronic or mechanical, including photocopying,
recording, or by any information storage and retrieval system, without
permission in writing from the publisher.

Atheneum
Macmillan Publishing Company
866 Third Avenue, New York, NY 10022

Text set by Arcata Graphics Kingsport, Kingsport, Tennessee
Printed and bound by Fairfield Graphics, Fairfield, Pennsylvania
Designed by Mary Ahern
First Edition

10 9 8 7 6 5 4 3 2 1

Library of Congress Cataloging-in-Publication Data

Hauptly, Denis J.
"A convention of delegates."

Bibliography: p. 140
SUMMARY: Describes the events occurring before and during the Constitutional
Convention, in which delegates from the thirteen original states
struggled to agree on a Constitution.
1. United States. Constitutional Convention (1787)—Juvenile literature.
2. United States—Constitutional history—Juvenile literature. [1. United States.
Constitutional Convention (1787) 2. United States—Constitutional history] I. Title.
KF4520.Z9H38   1987   342.73'029   86-17260
ISBN 0-689-31148-6   347.30229

To

Dr. Cleveland Williams

&

Dr. Henry Fairbanks

C O N T E N T S

"A CONVENTION OF DELEGATES"

The Creation of the Constitution

Introduction

Suppose a group of people came to you and said, "We would like to have a new government and we think that you are just the person to set it up for us!" Easy to imagine, maybe, but how would you begin? First you'd need to ask some questions. "How big a government would you like?" "What type of government would you prefer?" "What powers should the government have?" "What powers should the government not be allowed?"

When you had the answers to these and a hundred other questions you could sit down with a pencil and a lot of paper and begin to write what's called a constitution. A constitution is a group of laws, but not the sort you hear about every day. Your city council or Congress or Parliament passes many laws. Before they vote on these laws they don't usually ask you what you think. If you call or write they'll listen to what you have to say and they'll sometimes call you and ask for your opinion. But most of the time the lawmakers do the job pretty much by themselves. If you don't like the laws they approved, you can vote them out of office in the next election or work to get the laws repealed.

A constitution is different though. In its best sense, the constitution or charter of a place is a contract worked out by the people who live there. It controls the people who are elected or named to public offices and it can only be changed when the people agree that it should be changed. It is the basic law. It is the most powerful law.

Now let's imagine that you accepted the job of writing the constitution. You should know that your job's not going to be an easy one. Even if you asked very good questions, there are still going to be many little things that you didn't think of.

Let's say that the constitution is for a city. (Usually city constitutions are called charters.) And let's say that you were very clever and asked your visitors if they wanted to have a city council, and they did want one. You can't just write down on your paper that there will be a city council. You have to say more than that. How many members will there be? How will they be elected; from different districts in the city or from the city as a whole? How many votes will it take to pass a bill? If you say a majority vote wins, do you mean a majority of all the members at a meeting or a majority of all who were elected, even if some are missing from a certain meeting?

This isn't so easy. You might have to spend a few days on this and you might have to go back and ask many more questions.

Let's make things even more difficult. Let's say that you are writing this constitution with a large group of people—fifty or more. That means that you'll have to take votes on all the little problems that come up. And let's say that these fifty people come from very different backgrounds and have very different ideas on what the new government should be like. Let's really complicate things and say that some of these people don't even think that there should be a new government.

In a very simple form, this is the problem that the drafters of the Constitution of the United States had. They had to form a new government with very little advice from the people who were to be governed by it and do it even though they were not able to agree among themselves on what would be the wisest course.

The drafters were very lucky, though, for at the Constitutional Convention there were such people as George Washington, Benjamin Franklin, and James Madison. As we shall see, these people and others like them reached an agreement that was to last for more than 200 years.

What they did was one of the great events in American history, and it's a very important event in world history, too. Not only was a new nation about to be born, but also a new idea was about to be brought into the world: the idea that the people could run their own government. Strange as it may seem to us today, this was a very bold idea at the time. When the idea bore fruit and the new nation prospered and grew, the concept of democracy was not such a crazy one anymore, and the people of all the world could have hope of one day living under a government of their own choice.

This all began one day in 1787 in Philadelphia, Pennsylvania, but let us look back a few years earlier to find how the scene was set.

C H A P T E R

1

A Confederation
of States

The United States as we know it today had its birth in late December, 1783. The birthplace was not in Philadelphia or Boston but in Annapolis, Maryland. A man had ridden into town the day before to quit his job. He was uncommonly tall for his time—six feet, two inches in height. He had gray-blue eyes, chestnut-brown hair, powerful muscles, and unusually large hands and feet. He was not a handsome man, but he was a striking one. He was a man at whom people would stop and stare much as they might look closely at a professional athlete today, even if they did not know who he was.

But everyone knew who George Washington was. He had been one of the most famous men in the American colonies for the past twenty years, since he had been the most famous American commander in the French and Indian War. His fame had grown greater during the recent years when he had led the American army against the British in the revolutionary war.

That war was now over and America was free of British control, and soon George Washington would be free too— free to return to his beloved farm on the banks of the Potomac River in northern Virginia and to live the life of a planter. The next day he would resign as commander-in-chief of the army and announce that his life of public service was over. It was not over, of course. In fact, the most important years lay ahead. But this act of resigning his office was one of the most important things George Washington would ever do.

What's the big deal? you might ask. People quit their jobs every day, and what else was Washington going to do anyway? The war was over, and there's not much sense to being a general when there is no war. Washington always said that he wanted to go back and be a farmer again after the war, so he was just doing what he wanted to.

And that's the point. Washington was a man whose roots were in America. His family had come over from England three generations before. He himself had never been to England or any part of Europe. He was an American, and his generation was the first generation of real Americans. Many of them, like Washington, had no direct connections with the Old World. They had been raised in the New World by people who had themselves been raised in the New World. England and its kings and queens and parliaments was something they heard about from others. They might have read about some events in Europe in a newspaper if they could read and if they could get hold of a newspaper.

But they had other interests—American interests. They

George Washington was a leader in every area that he ever worked in—from surveying to politics. One author has rightly called him "the indispensable man."

had their own governments and their own problems. Every now and then, though, the problems of Europe would come to them. Washington had gained his first fame in the French and Indian War, which was an example of European problems visiting America. He gained his second fame in the American Revolution, which was caused in part by the English need to raise money through taxes on the American colonists.

Many people in America were like Washington. They had no strong feelings about England except when England bothered them. Before the Revolution, if asked, they would have said that they supported the king, but most would not have felt very deeply about it. Others felt differently. Perhaps they had been born in England or perhaps they ran a business that depended on English customers. These people were upset by the Revolution, and they felt very uneasy at its end. Others felt uneasy too. A revolution had been fought and won and the colonies were no longer ruled by a king. But who would they be ruled by? A mob? That crazy man Samuel Adams up in Boston? A democracy?

The word democracy is a very common one today, but there were no democracies when George Washington rode into Annapolis in 1783. There had once been some before, in ancient Greece, but few people were educated enough to know much about those governments, and those who were had no reason to believe that what had worked for a short time in some small cities in Greece two thousand years before would work in a new land in 1783.

Some of these people would have liked to have a king in America. To them the Revolution had not been fought to get rid of kings but to get rid of foreign kings—the ones in England. The man they wanted to be king was George Washington. He was a kingly man. At his back he had an army that supported him greatly. He had many reasons to be upset at the Congress that was a sort of government for America. They had not provided him with the supplies he had needed during the war and now, after the war, they refused to make good on promises they had made to reward the soldiers who had stood by Washington for so long and through such terrible struggles.

When Washington turned down those who asked him to take over the government of the colonies, he established the idea in people's minds that this new country, whatever it was going to be, was not going to be governed in the same way that Europe had been for centuries. This was not going to be a government of one man, but a government of all the people. At the moment he turned in his resignation, Washington literally decided the fate of America for many years to come.

There were others who would have liked to have been a king or queen and to have ruled over this wealthy new continent, but only Washington was supported by enough people and had the military strength to carry it off.

There is nothing in the record to show that Washington ever thought about it again. The moment came and passed, and he never looked back. That is a remarkable fact about the man, and it tells us as much about him as anything else in his life. More than any of the other heroes and heroines of early America, George Washington is a mystery to many people today. We know all about his great military feats and we know that he led America through some very difficult days in peacetime too. But who was he? How did he become the man he did become? What was he really like?

Washington never went to school as we know it today, but his writings show a very thoughtful man who was interested in many areas of knowledge. He was thought of as a very good athlete, as well. He is said to have had a good sense of humor. In the last year of his life, when he was ill and worried about money matters, he was told that there were not enough houses in the new city that would bear his name and become the nation's capital the next year. He thought that this was very funny and suggested that the senators and congressmen and the president could all camp out in the fields.

Was he ever nervous about all the important decisions he had to make and was he ever upset or sad when he turned out to be wrong? Certainly he must have had some lonely moments when no one else could understand the pressure that he was under, but the one great feature about him is that he seemed always to be in control. If his army was defeated or his plans for the government did not work out, he seemed to spend very little time worrying about his mistakes. Instead he looked to the future. He planned what he could do to make things work out better the next time.

He was above all else a leader—someone whom people would turn to in times of trouble and find a source of hope and strength. In those years from 1776 to the end of his Presidency in 1797, America needed him very often.

The need was just as great in 1783 as it had been during the Revolution. America was in trouble, whether it knew it or not. It was free, but it had been tied with England for a century and a half and it did not know how to make its way in the world without help. During the Revolution, when Washington had written to the Continental Congress about his great need for uniforms and food for his troops, the Congress had written back that during the earlier war (the French and Indian War) the soldiers had supplied their own clothes and food. They did not stop to think that the "earlier war" had been a small one and that most of the troops in it had either been British troops supplied by the British army or local militia who were fighting very close to their homes.

Now, during the Revolution, the job of supplying an army for all of the states was the job of the Congress, but at this time, when America needed money the most, much of its important trade was cut off because the British would not allow American ships in the West Indies.

The loss of trade with the West Indies was a serious blow to Congress for two reasons. First, the West Indies trade had been a very important source of money before the Revolution for all the colonies. Second, Congress had very limited powers to tax the states for the money it needed, and it depended on the duty (taxes) on trade.

America was run at the time under what were called the Articles of Confederation. These had been written during the Revolution and the separate states gave very little power to Congress. The different colonies had grown up almost as separate nations. Some were founded by Quakers, while others were started by Puritans or Anglicans. Some were almost entirely British, while others had large numbers of Germans or Dutch or Swedes. Some had slaves from Africa. In fact, while Africans made up 17 percent of the American population at the time of the Revolution, almost all of those Africans were in the Southern states, which meant that those states had a very high percentage of Africans in their population.

These and many other differences led the states to be very independent of each other and even to distrust each other a little. They found it hard to work together and very hard to work with each other on matters concerning money. The idea that each state ruled its own business was a basic belief, so, in the Articles of Confederation, the Continental Congress was not given the power to tax the people in the separate states. Instead Congress had to decide how much money it needed and then had to divide that amount among all the states. The way it proceeded was to ask each state how wealthy it was and to charge the wealthier states more than the poorer states. The trouble with that was that Congress had no way of knowing how wealthy each state really was. It had to take the word of the state itself.

If someone lived in New Hampshire and heard that Virginia claimed it was not as rich as he thought it was, then the person from New Hampshire might not trust the people from Virginia very much, and they in turn might not like the one from New Hampshire because the Virginians knew he didn't trust them. Some states did not pay taxes at all because their local legislatures could not agree on how much they should pay. As you can see, these assessments (as they were called) of the different states were not a very good way for Congress to raise the money it needed to pay for the army and to repay all of the money it owed from the revolutionary war.

Congress's other way of making money was to tax imports—goods brought in by ship from other countries. When the trade from the West Indies was cut off by the British, much of that money was cut off too. Even the small remaining amount of money was not certain, because the states with the biggest port cities often refused to vote for import taxes.

Congress had very little money and a very large debt because the costs of the Revolution were owed mostly by Congress, not by the states.

Money was not the only problem, though. There was the difficult question of trade between the states. Take a look at a map of the United States today. New Jersey is squeezed in between New York and Pennsylvania. Anything that New Jersey wanted to ship out for sale and to ship in to buy had to pass through one or the other of those states. If either state did not want it to go to or from New Jersey, it could stop it or tax it.

Suppose New Jersey wanted iron and it wanted to buy it from Virginia because Virginia had the lowest price. And suppose that Pennsylvania produced a lot of iron and wanted New Jersey to buy its iron and not Virginia's. It would tax the Virginia iron or even stop it from passing through Pennsylvania to force the people in New Jersey to buy iron in Pennsylvania.

That isn't very fair, but it was exactly what was happening under the Articles of Confederation because no one had the power to stop it. And even if Congress had been told that it had the power to govern trade between the states, it would not have been able to do it.

It's one thing to have a power under the law and another thing to put that power to work. To do so you need two things Congress didn't have: an executive branch of government to carry out its orders and national courts to settle any arguments about its powers.

Congress could pass a law, if it had the power, saying that no state could tax iron moving from one state to another. But if a state decided not to obey the order, who was going to stop it? The members of Congress were not going to go to Pennsylvania and arrest the governor or tax collector, and they were not going to sit as judges if people were charged with breaking the law. Without an executive and without judges, Congress had no real power to do even the very few things that the Articles of Confederation said that it could do.

This quick look at the Articles of Confederation shows three very serious problems. Congress could not really collect taxes. No one really had the power to control trade among the different states. And there was no one to carry out the laws Congress passed or to bring to justice those who would not obey those laws.

These problems are all in some way economic problems. That is, they are problems related to money or the use of money. The new nation had many economic problems to be sure, but it would be a mistake to say that the only problems were economic. There were other types of problems, too, and they are just as important in the story of the Constitutional Convention. The American people believed deeply in personal freedom. It was the reason that many of them or their ancestors had risked long and dangerous voyages across the Atlantic. But the new Confederation did not protect their freedoms if they traveled from state to state. If Massachusetts would not let Quakers own land, then a Quaker could not move to Massachusetts and buy a farm. If a citizen of South Carolina was injured by a citizen of Rhode Island, the person from South Carolina had to sue the person from Rhode Island in a Rhode Island state court before a judge and jury from Rhode Island.

There were problems, too, in dealing with foreign nations. England had not abandoned the New World after the Revolution. It had kept control of Canada, and the peace treaty ending the Revolution had allowed some time for England to move its troops out of posts on the American frontier. The British took longer than they were supposed to in doing this, and some people believed that their soldiers were stirring up trouble with the Indians on the frontier. Before the Revolution, the British had barred the American settlers from moving out into the lands past the Allegheny Mountains. After the war many Americans wanted to settle beyond the old boundaries, but fear of the British and worry about the Indians stopped them.

England was not the only nation causing trouble for the new nation. The Spanish claimed all land south of the Ohio River and controlled all traffic on the Mississippi River. The Americans in what was then called the West needed to be able to use the river to move the goods they made and grew, and the Spanish would not let them. There was a real danger that the western settlers would be forced into giving some territory over to the Spanish in order to protect their right to trade.

The Confederation did not work well economically. It did not work well in controlling the relationship between the states. It did not work well in protecting the rights of the people of all the states. And it did not work well in helping America to deal with foreign countries.

One of the first people to realize something had to be done was Alexander Hamilton. Hamilton had been Washington's chief aide during the revolutionary war and had seen the difficulties that Washington had had in trying to get Congress to answer his calls for help. In September of 1780 he had written to a friend: "There is only one remedy—to call a convention of all the states." Hamilton was a young and very stubborn man when he wrote those words, but it was to take much of his energy and all of his stubbornness over the next few years to reach his goal.

Although the problems of the Confederation were great and very real, they did not often bother the local farmer trying to raise crops and feed a family. Few people who had not been in Congress or the state legislatures realized how bad things really were. It would take years of educating and explaining before America would be ready to do anything as risky as starting a whole new form of government.

Even Washington, who knew more about the problems of the Confederation than anyone else, was not sure that major surgery was needed to cure those problems. In 1782 he sent around to friends and associates a letter in which he argued that there was a need for a strong national government, but that such a government could be created by reading broadly the terms of the Articles of Confederation, the laws that created and governed the Continental Congress.

Perhaps Washington felt that things would work out because he was now himself just a farmer. When he resigned from the army he told the Congress that he would never again accept a position in public office, and he meant it. When he returned to Mount Vernon he wrote to his friend and fellow soldier, the Marquis de Lafayette: "I am not only retiring from all public employments, but I am retiring within myself, and shall be able to view the solitary walk and tread the paths of private life with heartfelt satisfaction. . . . I will move gently down the stream of life until I sleep with my fathers."

The quiet life for Washington started before dawn with office work in the house, breakfast at 7:00 A.M., and then out to tour the large land holdings he had added to Mount Vernon. He would study the newest farming methods from Europe and he was working to breed a better mule.

He had a great interest in the western lands. As a very young man he had gone out to work as a surveyor in these unexplored areas and, just a few years later, commanded troops in the west during the French and Indian War. Now, in retirement, he went back again to look at some land that he had bought before the Revolution and was thinking of selling to pay off his debts. There, in the

West, Washington saw great opportunity and, without knowing it, brought himself right back into the middle of public life.

Remember that the Spanish had cut off American trade on the Mississippi and that the English still controlled lands west of the Allegheny Mountains. Within the British lands flowed the Ohio River, which farther to the west joined the Mississippi. The British would not let American goods travel west on the Ohio, and the river did not flow far enough east to bring the goods to the American markets on the coast. But Washington saw that if a route could be cut between the Ohio and the Potomac River and if the Potomac River could be made safe for ships by means of a canal, the markets on the American coast could be opened for western goods.

This idea offered much to the young nation. By providing American markets, the canal project would make the western settlers independent of the British and the Spanish. It would also make those markets and those who traded in them much wealthier. There was one big problem though. The canal project needed the cooperation of three states. Maryland and Virginia, which were on either side of the Potomac River, and Pennsylvania through which the final canal connection between the Ohio and the Potomac would be made.

In order to work out an agreement about the Potomac canal, representatives of Maryland and Virginia met at Mount Vernon in March of 1785. Under Washington's chairmanship, the two states worked out an agreement. The members were so pleased at the ease with which they had worked out their problems they agreed to hold such a meeting every year. The next meeting was to be held at Annapolis (giving that small city another reason to claim an important role in the creation of the Constitution). Maryland decided to expand the group by inviting Pennsylvania and Delaware. Virginia thought that was a good idea and decided to go Maryland one better and invite all thirteen states.

The meeting took place in September of 1786 and although only five of the thirteen states sent delegates, that small group took a very big step. They issued a call for a meeting the next May in Philadelphia to "render the constitution of the federal government adequate."

The Annapolis meeting was not the first to call for a gathering for such a purpose. A year before, young James Madison had moved in the Virginia legislature for a meeting of all the states, to authorize Congress to govern trade and collect taxes. But the resolution in Annapolis had a different ring to it. These people were talking about a new government, not a patched-up version of the old Articles of Confederation.

Not everybody favored such an idea. In fact, at the Annapolis meeting the Maryland delegation did not take part because of a fear that even this meeting would take away from the authority of the Congress.

Congress was aware of the sad state of the national government, and should have called for the meeting, but hadn't done so. Instead, a small group meeting on its own had made the call. If Congress did nothing, it would look silly and probably ruin whatever chances the meeting had of success. If Congress voted against the meeting, it would be saying that everything was fine, and the members knew that was not true. If Congress voted for the meeting, it would give its approval to a meeting whose purposes were not entirely clear.

Congress took the careful way out and, in February, 1787, it approved a "convention of delegates" to meet in Philadelphia in May of that year "for the sole and express purpose of revising the Articles of Confederation."

The convention was to meet none too soon. In the summer and fall of 1786, a group of farmers in western Massachusetts under the leadership of Daniel Shays had rebelled against high taxes and the taking of their farms for debts. The rebellion did not last long, but it had the leaders of the new nation very worried. If Americans started fighting among themselves, the foreign nations that were still interested in the New World might take advantage of it.

Washington had not attended the Annapolis meeting because of his vow to stay out of public life, and he was not going to go to Philadelphia for the same reason. But Shays's Rebellion caused his friends to urge him to change his mind. The Convention had to succeed. If it did not, all that Washington had fought for and believed in might die. If Washington stayed home, the one person whom all people and all parties trusted would be absent, and many would say that his absence showed that he did not approve of what the Convention was doing. If Washington went, his presence could make a real difference.

It was a matter of duty, and as always Washington responded to the call.

CHAPTER

2

A Chronicler of Events

Almost every account by someone who had met or seen George Washington begins the same way: by mentioning his size. He was a very large man for his time, and his bearing, the way he carried himself, made him seem even larger than he actually was.

Almost every account of James Madison also begins with a mention of his size, for Madison was a short man for his time. He was very slim, with a boyish face and a very soft voice.

Not only were Washington and Madison different in size; they were also very different in reputation. Madison had a local reputation in Virginia and in Congress as a very bright young fellow who wrote rather well. The same could be said for a hundred other people. There was only one George Washington.

Washington was the greatest of all war heroes in America, its greatest leader in the French and Indian War and in the Revolution. Madison had been too sickly to fight during the Revolution. Washington received his slight education at home. Madison had gone to Princeton University.

Madison was called Jamie by those who knew him. Washington was addressed as General, even by his wife. Madison dressed in black and had a quiet social life. Washington was a very social man, who was the center of attention at parties and whose house was always filled with unexpected guests.

But although these two men were so very different—twenty years apart in age and two hundred years apart in experience—yet Madison must be ranked as an equal with George Washington in the creation of the new government. Washington was the heart behind the new nation. He dreamed the dream and did the daily work that was needed. He spoke and others followed. At the Convention, at least, James Madison was the mind of America.

Madison was born near Port Royal, Virginia, in March of 1751. His family had been in America for nearly 100 years, and so, like Washington, his connections with England were very weak. His family had settled frontier lands in the Tidewater region of Virginia, and by the time Madison was born the family was centered around the great estate of Montpelier. Though they owned large areas of land, his family was not wealthy. Life was too hard on the frontier. All supplies had to be brought in from the outside, often from England. All the goods that the farm produced had to be taken by wagon to the ports along the James River.

The family was comfortable enough, though, to see to it that young James was well educated for his time. He was first trained at home by his grandmother and mother, who taught him to read and write. Then, when he was

James Madison, who was called by many "The Father of the Constitution."

eleven years old, he was sent to King and Queen County, Virginia, where he was enrolled in the boarding school run by Donald Robertson. Robertson was a Scotsman and a university graduate. He was also apparently a very good teacher.

The first year Madison studied languages and mathematics. The next year he concentrated on Latin and was soon reading the great Roman poets and philosophers. As he reached the age when most children today start high school, Robertson introduced him to Montesquieu, Locke, and Descartes. These were the leading thinkers of Europe, and leaders, also, in the movement that came to be known as the Enlightenment.

The thinkers of the Enlightenment were greatly interested in the writings of the past with the purpose of applying the best ideas about government and science to the world of the mid-1700s. In many ways they were reacting against the rigid governments and sloppy science of the time. The men and women of the Enlightenment took a new look at the world around them, but they did so with a very good knowledge of what had been tried and had failed or succeeded in the past.

Having been exposed to all these ideas, Madison finished at Donald Robertson's school a well-educated young man. But when he returned home, he studied for two more years with the Episcopal minister in his town and then was admitted to Princeton University, which was known as the College of New Jersey. This was an unusual choice, for most good students from his area went to the College of William and Mary in Williamsburg, Virginia. Madison chose Princeton partly because the religious views of that college were closer to his family's liberal opinions than were those at William and Mary. Partly he went there because he was already regarded as a sickly person, and William and Mary was thought to have an unhealthy climate. The climate at Princeton must have been very good indeed because Madison lived to be eighty-five years of age.

Madison was a bright student and finished at Princeton in two years instead of the normal four. He graduated in 1771, a year when the first murmurings of revolution were being heard in the American colonies. The French and Indian War had ended in 1763. In Europe, war between the French and the English had been replaced by commercial rivalry. The Enlightenment was reaching toward its full bloom. European chemists were unlocking the secrets of the elements, having produced hydrogen and oxygen in their laboratories. In the more practical sciences, the invention of the spinning jenny and the steam engine had set the stage for the Industrial Revolution.

It was a time of great change, and as science began to understand how to control the physical world, political philosophers tried to do the same to the world of government. Of the many complaints that the colonists had against the British, most had to do with trade and trade policies. Looking back, these often seem to us to be very small things to start a war about. But though the arguments were made in terms of pounds and pence, the more important questions of self-government were what lay beneath these money questions. The most direct contact that the colonists had with the British government was through taxes and import duties. If the British could rule the colonists with an iron hand on these matters, could they someday tell them what their newspapers could print and what religion they had to follow?

The colonists were too independent to let that happen. They had grown to love the freedom the Atlantic Ocean gave them. It had kept the British out of their daily lives by slowing down communication. An act of rebellion in the colonies might take two months to get reported to London, and another two months might pass before the British government could respond. So when the British started to control tightly ways that the Americans could buy and sell their goods and where they could do it, it was easy for the American colonists to agree to protest the British actions.

One of the main weapons they used was the boycott. All over the colonies people met and agreed that they would not buy British goods and that they would encourage their neighbors to boycott the British as well. Actually, *encourage* is not the right word. They encouraged their neighbors by striking fear in their hearts, by burning their shops, by listing their names in the newspapers if they did deal in British goods, and by other strong measures.

Shortly after Madison returned home from Princeton, he became a member of one of these enforcement groups and, though only twenty-three at the time, his reputation as a leader in his community grew.

War came quickly as the Americans put more and more pressure on the British and the British refused to back down. Madison didn't fight in the war, but climbed rapidly on the political ladder. He served in the Virginia legislature and then he was elected to the Continental Congress in 1780. At twenty-nine, he was its youngest member. Madison stayed quiet for the first six months; he had a reputation for being very smart and a little shy. When he finally did speak, it was on an unusual subject for someone from a landholding Virginia family. The subject was slavery.

It had become very hard to keep soldiers in the American army. Many were being asked to fight far away from their home colonies and to stay away from home during important parts of the farming year. Congress was interested in finding ways to keep the troops enlisted in the army. One plan that was proposed would give a slave to each soldier who reenlisted. That way the soldier-farmer would be able to stay in combat while the slave took care of the farming chores. Madison proposed another way of dealing with the shortage of soldiers. He suggested that the slaves who had been freed be asked to join together to form black regiments to fight the British. Madison's plan was passed by the Congress and the black fighting groups were formed.

The years in Congress were good preparation for Madison's future work in the Constitutional Convention. He learned much about the way in which legislative bodies operate, and the Convention was really a legislative body. It was a group of people brought together to draft a law. Each of its members had equal powers, and each had his own ideas about what the Constitution should be. Not all of these ideas could be written into the Constitution.

In fact, as we shall see, some of these ideas were in conflict with each other.

In Congress, Madison learned the importance of compromise and he learned how to do it. It would be the compromises between conflicting ideas that would make the Convention a success.

Madison also learned firsthand the defects of the Articles of Confederation. He saw the ways in which the government failed to work properly and had some thoughts as to how those problems could be cured. But many members of the Convention had been members of Congress, and they had as much knowledge of the difficulties as did Madison. The real strength that he brought to the Convention was not his answers to these old problems but his vision of what the future government should be like.

When Madison was selected to be one of Virginia's delegates to the Convention, he immediately wrote to Thomas Jefferson, who at that time was serving as the American ambassador in Paris. Jefferson was among the most widely read of all Americans, and Madison asked him to send him some books to read in preparation for the great work ahead of him. Asking Thomas Jefferson to send some books was like hoping for some snow and getting a blizzard. Jefferson sent him hundreds of books. He sent him more books than most people read in a lifetime and Madison had only a few months before the Convention.

James Madison must have worked very hard at his reading. By the end of April, 1787, he had prepared two papers to bring with him to the Convention. One was called "Of Ancient and Modern Confederacies." It was a study of different governments past and present. They were compared with each other and with the American government. The second was titled "Vices of the Political System of the United States." It was a study of the defects of the Articles of Confederation.

Madison left New York, where Congress was meeting, for Philadelphia on May 2, 1787. That was almost a month before the Convention was to begin. He was getting to Philadelphia early because he was very excited by the idea of the Convention. He wanted to be there from the very first moment and not to miss a thing. He had nothing to worry about because he was the first to arrive and none of the others showed up for eleven days.

The delegates who were to follow in a few days were a distinguished group. Of the fifty-five of them, eight had been among the signers of the Declaration of Independence, seven had been governors of their states, three-fourths had served in Congress, twenty-one had fought in the Revolution. They were not all native Americans. In fact nine of them had been born in other countries. A new government for a nation composed of many different peoples was to be formed by a group of men with very different backgrounds.

They had some things in common, though. They were all men. Women had very limited rights at this time and the right to vote (and to hold office) was not among them. They were also all white. Although there were a fairly large number of freed slaves in the new nation, very few of these had been granted the right to vote. While they were "free," they were limited in their opportunities by

This is a view of Philadelphia a few years before the Convention. Although it gives the appearance of a large city, most of the buildings were along the water, and it was actually little more than a small town.

lack of education and property. The ownership of land was generally necessary to have the right to vote in those days. It was felt that a person who owned land had a stronger personal interest in the actions of the government than someone who did not. Few blacks owned enough land to qualify as voters.

The delegates were not poor or even average Americans. Most of them were prosperous men whose financial success had given them a reputation in their states and had allowed them to take time off from the needs of daily living to serve in their state legislatures or in the Congress. They were an American aristocracy. But in a sense they were a revolutionary aristocracy. After all, they had overthrown British rule at the risk of their own lives and fortunes. They were not among that large group of wealthy Americans who had supported the British. They believed in the new nation. Jefferson called them "an assembly of demigods."

Jefferson may have been a little too generous. Another writer described them more accurately:

the convention as a whole was composed of men such as would be appointed to a similar gathering at the present time: professional men, business men, and gentlemen of leisure; patriotic statesmen and clever, scheming politicians; some trained by experience and study for the task before them, and others utterly unfit. It was essentially a representative body, taking possibly a somewhat higher tone from the social conditions of the time, the seriousness of the crisis, and the character of the leaders.

They were young. Their average age was only forty-two. Since most of them had been in Congress, they were probably more knowledgeable about their fellow-countrymen than other Americans were. They had traveled and had learned of the problems of regions outside their own. It was a good group. Its views and the law it produced would be respected by most Americans. They had a chance to succeed at the very difficult mission that was ahead of them. Few of them suspected how really difficult it was to be.

Madison waited for his company. The other delegates started to arrive in the middle of May, but the Convention rules as set down by Congress required that a majority of the thirteen states be represented before the Convention started. Each state made its own rule about when it was "represented." Some states held that one delegate would be enough to cast the state's vote. (Each state would have one vote in the Convention and could send as many delegates as it wanted; the vote of the delegation would determine how the state cast its single vote.) Other states had required that two or three delegates be present before the state would be "represented."

On May 25, 1787, a quorum of seven state delegations was finally present and the Convention opened. The Convention met at Pennsylvania's State House. This was the same building where the Declaration of Independence had been signed eleven years before. The room assigned to the Convention was a large one. It was square and measured forty feet to a side and had a ceiling that soared twenty feet over the delegates' heads. There were windows on two sides of the room. These would be needed, because the summer ahead was to be one of the hottest in recent memory. As the summer grew hotter, the windows were kept open and the noise from the street below disrupted the Convention's meetings. Finally, dirt had to be spread on the street to quiet the pounding of the horses' hooves and the creaking of the wagon wheels.

Around the room were a number of desks for the dele-

Independence Hall in Philadelphia was the site of the Constitutional Convention.

gates. They sat at these in groups of three or four. Though there were fifty-five official delegates, there were rarely more than thirty at any given meeting. The absences were not always caused by lack of interest in the Convention but often by the fact that individual delegates were needed at home or had personal business to attend to. The Convention met each day at 10:00 A.M. and usually recessed for the day at three in the afternoon.

Most of the delegates were from out of town, of course, and so each had to find a place to stay. Many of them chose the Indian Queen Tavern on nearby Fourth Street. That was to become a center for informal meetings of the delegates. The delegates from a state would often meet someplace outside the Convention to try to settle any differences they might have and so present a united position at the Convention itself.

On the morning of Friday, May 25, Madison entered the hall and carefully selected a desk in the center of the front row. He was determined to take careful notes of the debates, and he wanted to be in a position where he could catch every word. He was the most faithful delegate at the convention, missing only a few minutes at a time and never missing more than an hour altogether. It is from Madison's notes that we have most of our knowledge of what went on. The rules of the Convention required secrecy, and no one was allowed to talk about the debates to outsiders. Even Madison's notes were kept from public view until his death, nearly fifty years after the Convention had ended.

Of course the Convention did not just start. It had to

organize itself, and the right of members to sit had to be checked. Each delegation had what are called "credentials." Credentials are documents that show the right of the parties carrying them to represent some other party or government.

The delegations each presented their credentials, which were read out loud. Normally, this is a very simple matter, but the reading of the credentials at the Constitutional Convention provided an early clue to some of the problems that would have to be faced. One problem arose when the credentials of the Delaware delegation were read. The legislature of that state had laid a condition on its delegates. They were ordered to not approve any document that would change the part of the Articles of Confederation that stated that, in Congress, each state, no matter what its size, would have only one vote. The matter was important to Delaware because it was a small state and if each state were to have votes in Congress equal to its population, large states, such as New York and Virginia, could easily outvote Delaware or any of the small states.

The Delaware problem doubtless caused a good deal of buzzing among the delegates. Another matter in the order of business would be much easier. The Convention needed a head, a president. There was only one man for the job and that was George Washington. He had the respect of all, and his fairness had never been doubted. He was used to leading. He was an early supporter of the idea of the Convention, and he was the one person who could sell the Convention's work to the American people. He was to have been nominated by Benjamin

Franklin, but it was rainy that day and that great, but now very old man had been kept at home. Instead, Washington was nominated by Robert Morris. The vote was unanimous in his favor.

Even a man as trusted as Washington needed a set of rules to apply. So the Convention created a Committee on Rules that was to meet over the weekend and to report back with a set of rules for the Convention to operate under. The Convention then adjourned to await the committee's report.

On Monday morning George Wythe of Virginia rose to present the proposed rules. Wythe had founded the law school at William and Mary College and was one of the leading legal thinkers in America. The basic rules he read out were simple enough for anyone to understand.

Speakers were always to talk to the president of the Convention, not to their fellow delegates. They were not to be interrupted. No delegate could make more than two speeches on any particular subject without special permission from the Convention. This rule was intended to allow the president to stop long-winded delegates from tying up the Convention and to force the delegates to think carefully before speaking on any subject. The second speech on a subject could not be given by a delegate until all others had had the chance to make their first speech.

Seven states would make up a quorum so that the Convention could do business. A vote would be won by a majority of those states present. For instance, if only nine states were represented on a certain day and a vote came up, the issue would be decided by the vote of five states.

If all thirteen states were present, the vote of seven would be needed to win. This was a somewhat harsh rule, since there was the possibility that some important issues could be decided by the votes of only four states (a majority of a quorum of seven states). To soften that possibility, the next rule provided that all votes could be brought up for reconsideration at a later time.

Finally, the rules committee recommended that all votes be recorded, but that the results of the votes and all other Convention matters be kept secret from the public so that the Convention could not be influenced by the outside world.

The rules were adopted, and on that last Monday in May the Constitutional Convention began its business. The path ahead was unclear. No one knew what the Convention would really do or how long it would take to do it.

The Convention had a leader and a historian. What it needed now was a map to follow. The next day it would have one.

CHAPTER
3
The Virginia Plan

On May 29, 1787, a man named Edmund Randolph stood up to address the Constitutional Convention. He had a plan to offer. The Virginia delegates had been meeting while they waited for the other delegations to arrive and they had a proposal they thought would be useful as a starting point for the Convention's debates.

Randolph's selection as the person to present the Virginia Plan was a great honor and had come to Randolph after a career of important honors. He had been an aide to General Washington, a very successful lawyer, a judge, a member of the Virginia legislature, a member of Congress, the attorney general of Virginia, and now he was the governor of that large state. He was only thirty-three years old.

Everyone has heard of George Washington and James Madison, and some other people at the Convention are very familiar to us today. But if you go through the list of all of the delegates at the end of this book, you'll find many whose names mean nothing to you at all. In a very few cases that's because they were people who really never accomplished anything in their lives except being a delegate to the Convention. Even at the Convention they did very little. The Convention was not a body of perfect men. It had its share of self-important loudmouths who would give long and useless speeches on any subject at any time.

But the general quality of the Convention was so high that a few people of real importance at the Convention and in their time are not well remembered 200 years later. We'll meet a few of these people in this book, and Edmund Randolph is the first of them.

The Randolph family was among the most important in Virginia. It was far more important in its time than such families as the Madisons or Washingtons. Edmund's father was John Randolph. He had been the attorney general of Virginia, as had his father and his brother before him. John Randolph had been educated in the finest legal training school in the English-speaking world, the Inns of Court in London.

In 1751, John Randolph returned from England to the family home in Williamsburg, Virginia, and married Ari-anna Jennings, the daughter of the attorney general of Maryland. Their son, Edmund, was born in Williamsburg on August 10, 1753. Edmund received a fine education for his time. He attended the grammar school run by the College of William and Mary. The training was classical and the hours were long. Classes ran from seven in the morning to six at night. In 1770 he started classes at the college itself and had nearly the best grades in his class. For some reason, though, he quit college just three months

Edmund Randolph had become one of the most important men in America while still in his early thirties, but his career ended in scandal.

before he was to graduate and started studying law under his father.

Whatever he learned in the classroom, his politics and government were learned at home. He lived in the capital of his state and his father and his uncle, Peyton Randolph, were deeply involved in the government. They were not in complete agreement, though. His uncle was a strong supporter of colonists' rights. When the British imposed special taxes on Americans, his uncle headed the protest committee that prepared a petition against those taxes. But Edmund's father refused to sign the petition.

The late 1760s and early 1770s must have been a very exciting time to be in Williamsburg and eating dinner with the leading citizens of that city. Revolution was in the air, but many people, like Edmund's father, still had strong loyalties to the crown. After the Boston Tea Party in 1774, another protest petition was circulated among the leading citizens. Again John Randolph refused to sign it.

The situation then must have been very difficult. As hard as it may be for us to accept 200 years later, the colonists' cause was not perfectly just, and the English position was not completely unjustified. People like John Randolph could feel deep sympathy for the problems of their fellow colonists but at the same time strongly oppose any break with England. Many important families and friendships were destroyed then. George Washington's closest friends, the Fairfaxes, returned to England just before the Revolution. Benjamin Franklin's son broke with his father and supported the British actively during the Revolution. John and Arianna Randolph felt the storm coming and felt that they could not be a part of it. In September of 1775 they set sail for England, never to return.

Earlier, when fighting broke out in April of 1775, Edmund had been forced to make a choice. All of Virginia knew that his father would not support the Revolution and that his uncle Peyton strongly supported the break from England. Edmund sided with his uncle and rebellion. Letters were written on his behalf to General Washington, who had just taken command of the American army in Boston. One of them suggested that young Edmund wanted to make up for his father's "misconduct."

Washington listened to those who supported Edmund's request for a position on his staff and named the twenty-one-year-old as an aide-de-camp. Edmund was to serve as a personal assistant and secretary to the general. He arrived in July and showed great interest in his new duties. But those duties were to last for only a few months.

Peyton Randolph, Edmund's uncle, died suddenly in October. When Edmund's father had left for England he had placed Peyton in charge of his financial matters. With Peyton's death, Edmund was needed at home to take care of both his father's and his uncle's estates.

Even with his brief service, Edmund was something of a hero when he came home. He had a famous name. Despite family opposition, he had joined General Washington's staff. And he was seen as a young man with a very bright future. Almost immediately after he came home he was named a judge of the Admiralty Court. His experience in the law, including all of his training under his father, did not amount to more than a few months. Becoming a judge was not the usual way to start a legal career. But Edmund did not stop there. Very soon he also became a member of the Virginia legislature. By May he had become the attorney general of Virginia. He was only twenty-three years old. In the United States today very few people finish law school before the age of twenty-four.

As if this were not enough activity for one person, Randolph also found the time to fall in love with and marry Elizabeth Nicholas, the daughter of another important Virginia family and a woman whom Edmund had known since childhood. By November he had been elected mayor of Williamsburg and a few months later was chosen to head the board of governors of William and Mary College.

This is all remarkable, and as you will see, the career of Edmund Randolph was just beginning. It takes nothing away from Randolph to point out that a war was on and there were very few lawyers to serve the Virginia government. Many who had not gone off to become officers in the Continental Army opposed the rebellion. Only men could hold public office, and anyone who opposed the Revolution could not be elected or appointed to any important position. Randolph was in the right place at the right time and he served in a large number of positions he might otherwise have had to wait for.

All of these positions were local positions, however. They were important in Virginia, of course, but they gave him no exposure to national politics, to the issues around which the Constitution would be formed. Randolph was serving as the Speaker of the Virginia Assembly in 1779 when he was chosen to be a member of the Continental

Congress. There he came into contact with people from other states and with other points of view. In Congress he worked on issues of trade with other countries and the regulation of commerce in the colonies, and from those experiences he could see that the loose structure under which the war-torn new nation was governed was not working very well.

He also now began to think of himself as an American. Like Madison and Washington, he had come from Virginia, where he was a man of great importance and he had grown up thinking that the greatest honors available to him would be in the service of his colony. Now the world was changing quickly and some people would not want or be able to keep up with the changes. His own parents had been among those who decided not to change. They had continued to define themselves in the old way: as English citizens who happened to have lived in a colony that was called Virginia.

For Randolph the change was more difficult than for others, perhaps because of his parents. During the years to come, and especially during the Convention, his positions would change often.

Because of the knowledge Edmund Randolph had gained about trade among the states from his experience in Congress, he was very interested in a special meeting Maryland and Virginia held in 1782. The purpose of the meeting was to work out a plan for the joint defense against the British of the great Chesapeake Bay, which touches both of those states. The interests of the two states were broader than this, as they soon realized.

In 1784 the two states held another meeting. By this time the war was over and the meeting was to focus on regulation of commerce along the Potomac River, also part of their boundary, and its development with a canal into a major highway of trade. As we know from Chapter One, many Virginians, including George Washington, were interested in such a plan. Randolph attended. By this time, he was not only attorney general of the state, but also, since the end of the war, he had established the largest private law practice in Virginia. The meeting was so successful a third one was called for Annapolis in 1786.

We have already seen something of that meeting when we talked about George Washington. The Annapolis Convention included more states and ended with a call for a national convention in Philadelphia to reform the Articles of Confederation. Randolph drafted the document calling for that meeting.

The new meeting was planned to go beyond the simple questions of trade among the states, which had been the subject of the earlier gatherings. It was to take a close look at all of the issues involved in governing the newly independent states. To reach that goal it was important that each state send its delegation with broad powers to approve changes. There were no jets or speedy trains in those days. If the delegates in Philadelphia were to find it necessary to go back home for more instructions, the work of the convention would be delayed for months or even years.

Randolph and his fellow Virginians realized this, so they worked hard to make sure that the Virginia delegation, at least, had the authority it needed. Randolph also worked hard to make sure that the state's and the nation's leading citizen, George Washington, would be in attendance. Randolph shared the view of many others that without Washington in Philadelphia the convention would not succeed. He wrote to the general in December of 1786, informing him that he had been selected as a delegate. Washington wrote a polite but firm letter back, repeating the position that he had announced at the end of the war that he would not again participate in public affairs. He was not going to break that promise.

As we have seen, Randolph was not alone in urging Washington to change his mind, and in April the general gave in to the pressure of his friends and the love of his country and agreed to join the delegation. In early May, Randolph set off for Philadelphia. He arrived on May 15, 1787, one of the last of the Virginians to appear. They began to meet for several hours a day, getting ready for the great events that lay before them.

The meetings were fruitful. The Virginia Plan, as the result of the meetings was called, was probably the work of James Madison. Certainly it had been approved by George Washington. There were two reasons Edmund Randolph was chosen to present it to the Convention. First of all Randolph was the governor of Virginia and as such he was the head of its delegation to the Convention, so the job was his because of his position. Also, Randolph was known as a strong debater. He would explain the Virginia position clearly and be ready for any opposition.

There was certain to be opposition, for the plan that Randolph was presenting was a very radical one. On the first formal business day of the Convention it would put to rest the idea that the Convention was meeting for the purpose of putting a few patches on the old Articles of Confederation. It was not just there to deal with the "national" problems of trade, taxation, and relations with other countries. The Virginia Plan would change the very design of national government. Each issue that troubled the new nation probably could have been solved if Congress had enough power. The Virginia Plan went well beyond dealing with those few issues and proposed a new form of government entirely, of which Congress was only one part.

Careful lawyer that he was, though, Randolph did not just stand up on the Convention floor and read off the plan. There might have been a second American Revolution in the hall had he done that. He started slowly, building a foundation to prepare his audience for the new government that he was going to propose.

He started by describing an ideal form of government; one in which the nation would have both security from interference by other nations and a sense of cooperation among citizens inside the country. He went on to describe the system of government under the Articles of Confederation, and the weaknesses in that form of government were highlighted against the ideal government he had spoken of. He warned, too, of the dangers of democracy, for Shays's Rebellion was in everybody's mind. While almost all of the delegates would have agreed that Shays and his followers had illustrated some basic faults in the national government, no one would have agreed that the opinions of Shays and his followers should rule the country.

"Democracy" was almost a bad word in those days. It seemed to many to mean only mob rule. For that reason, as we have noted, in the main only property owners who were white and male could vote. The Founding Fathers generally believed that was the way things should be. So Randolph's warning against democracy let them know that he thought the way they did. Whatever else they might think of the plan that he was to introduce, he did not want them to think that he was proposing democracy.

What he actually was proposing was strange enough to many of their ears. In fifteen sections, his proposal laid out a plan of government quite different from the one Americans had grown used to. Congress would have two houses. The lower house, the House of Representatives, would be elected by the people with the number of members from each state to be decided by population. The upper house, the Senate, would be chosen by the lower house from among candidates nominated by the state legislatures. The number of senators would also depend on the population of the state.

Congress would pass the laws. The national executive would carry them out. He was to be chosen by Congress and would serve for seven years. In addition to being the head of the executive branch of the government, the national executive would have the right to veto or cancel the laws passed by Congress after he had gotten the agreement of some Federal judges.

Most important, and most startling of all, was the fact that the new national government would be supreme. Its laws could override the laws of the different states. There was to be one national government and the thirteen states would be parts within it.

That seems perfectly normal to us today, in many state legislatures, however, the very mention of such an idea might well have set off a chorus of boos. But that did not happen. In fact, after Randolph presented the plan, a Pennsylvania delegate by the name of Gouverneur Morris moved that the Convention agree that "a national government ought to be established consisting of a supreme Legislative, Executive, and Judiciary." It may be that the delegates were all men of unusual wisdom and open-mindedness. It may be that they were so shocked by the scope of the Virginia Plan that they found it easy to accept any idea that did not go quite so far. It may be that Randolph was in top form and had carried the Convention along with him. Or it could be that the Virginia delegates had knocked on a few doors and talked with a number of delegates before the vote.

Whatever the reasons, and all of those listed are probably true to some degree, the Convention voted six to one (only seven states had full delegations at the time) to adopt Morris's proposal. In a sense, the Convention's work was over on that very first vote. It had decided what type of government the new nation would have—a national government. Everything else was just a matter of detail. But how they would fight over those details!

They had good reason to fight too. The details were

very important. It was one thing to create a national government. It was another thing to create that government in such a way that the majority of people would happily support it. Without support, the new government would be doomed.

The major battle was just ahead. You may remember that the Delaware delegates came to the Convention with instructions to vote only for a plan that would continue the practice of giving each state an equal vote in the Congress. Delaware was a small state both in area and population, and it feared that if each state had votes in Congress according to its population, a few large states would be in control of the entire nation.

Delaware was not alone in its fear. There were other small states that had the same concern. But proportional representation (the number of seats in Congress determined by the population of the state) was exactly what Edmund Randolph had proposed. Delaware could not vote for such a plan. Many other delegations would not vote for it. The idea of a national government was wonderful. But there were local concerns, too, and these the delegates would fight about them for weeks to come.

CHAPTER

4

The New Jersey Plan

Until now we have dealt with a limited group of people. They were native-born Americans from Virginia. We could spend a lot of time with those people because they were a very talented group. In fact, we have not really talked about Thomas Jefferson (because he was not at the Convention) and he was the most talented Virginian of all. It's hard to sit back and look at this time in American history and not be dazzled by these Virginians. They were bright. They were skilled politicians. They were educated in the classics. They were good speakers, and they were good writers. They had planned the Convention down to the first day. They knew what they wanted to achieve.

But they were not the United States. Their views were colored by local interests. They were human. Their plan for America would not work for the very simple reason that it was *their* plan. It was not America's plan, a scheme upon which all could and would agree. Certainly there would be opposition.

It is the glory of the Convention that the opposition

was not on a small point. It was on a very big point. The question was one of representation.

Representation was a big issue because it meant power in the new government. It was a big issue because the method selected for representation would define the character of the new government. If each state were to be given a representation in Congress according to its population, that would mean that the new government would be like a democracy. If each state were allowed an equal number of members of Congress, the result would be an assembly of states, each of which regarded itself as a country. This would be a kind of United Nations model in which a state with 50,000 citizens would claim equal status with a state with 1 million people.

The Virginia Plan proposed what is called proportional representation. The large states, like Virginia, would favor proportional representation because it gave them more votes in the national legislature. The small states, of course, would favor equal representation, which had been the rule under the Articles of Confederation and was the rule at the Constitutional Convention itself.

Now that the Virginia Plan had been put before the Convention, the small states had to step forward and argue their interests. Their chief spokesman in this task was William Paterson of New Jersey.

Paterson was born in what is now Northern Ireland in the year 1745. He was not wealthy. His father, Richard, had been a tinsmith in Ireland. In 1747 he brought the family to the New World. They moved around a bit at first, but by 1750 they had settled in Princeton, New Jersey.

The promise of the New World came true for Richard Paterson. He opened a general store in Princeton. The store was a good business, and Richard took his profits and invested them in land. The family did not become wealthy, but they were comfortable enough to send William to a private school in 1757. The school was founded by Aaron Burr, the father of the man who later became vice-president of the new nation and who was one day to kill Alexander Hamilton in a duel.

William learned Greek and Latin at Burr's school. Those classical languages were required for anyone who wanted to become a student at what was then called the College of New Jersey—now Princeton—the same school James Madison had attended.

William must have learned his lessons well. In 1759, at the age of fourteen, he entered Princeton. Actually, while most people enter college today when they are eighteen, young Paterson's age was fairly normal for his time. His studies at Princeton were in two areas. He took many courses in history and many in English literature. He developed a strong belief in simple language. Many of the writers of his time were very, very fancy. They used unusual words and long phrases to state simple thoughts. From his earliest student days, Paterson rejected this style. The clearness and simplicity of his language would make him a very effective writer and speaker.

William earned his undergraduate degree in 1763 (the same year that George Washington was fighting the French in the wilderness). He stayed at the university for three more years to take a master's degree. He had lived in

William Paterson was born in Northern Ireland, but he grew up in New Jersey and was educated at Princeton.

Princeton for nineteen years and in that time he had not traveled beyond the nearby city of Philadelphia.

That did not make him much different from Madison or Hamilton. Travel was difficult in those days. Even someone like Paterson who had crossed the Atlantic Ocean in a small wooden ship would not be very knowledgeable about the people one hundred miles away in the New World. Paterson grew up knowing only a little bit about life in New Jersey. Certainly, at Princeton, he must have met and dealt with people from the other colonies, but he had not seen their homes. He did not know what their daily problems were. His view of the world was as narrow as that of most other people living in the colonies then, even though he was very well educated.

One thing that he did know is that he wanted to be important. Today we would call Paterson a social climber. That is, he was a person who sought out wealthy and important friends in the hope that they would be useful to him in later life. America was a nation of social climbers. While some wealthy people had come over to settle in the New World, most of the colonists were ordinary people. In America the fact that one had been a tinsmith in Ireland did not matter much. A nation was being carved out of wilderness and what one did was more important than who one was.

Paterson's path to power was the law. There were no law schools in New Jersey at the time. The tradition was that a student would find a lawyer who was willing to let him read his law books and spend some time talking with him about the law. After a few years the lawyer would write a statement about the student to the courts. If they were satisfied that the young student had spent enough time and effort at his studies, they would admit him to the bar.

That pattern, called "reading law," held for the most part, until this century. In fact, there are still some American states where persons can be admitted to the bar by studying law in Paterson's way rather than by going to law school.

Paterson studied under Richard Stockton, a well-known lawyer who would later become a justice of the New Jersey Supreme Court. In 1768 Paterson was admitted to the bar in New Jersey.

He began his practice in the rural New Jersey counties of Hunterdon and Somerset. Like most young lawyers in those days, there were no law firms for him to join. He had to start his own practice and find his own clients. That meant pretty slim living for a few years. But Paterson had made important friends and they did help him out. In 1769 he was appointed to be a surrogate. These were lawyers who were paid by the state to represent it in cases concerning wills. If a person dies without leaving any heirs behind and without a will, his or her property goes to the state. Thus the state had an interest in many cases.

The surrogate work kept Paterson alive, but just barely. In 1772, he moved north in New Jersey to Raritan. There he opened a branch of his father's store. At that time, most of his law business consisted of defending his father in a series of suits.

Neither Paterson's law business nor his father's store were doing very well. But Paterson was impressing people anyway. The times were changing. The problems with England had grown greater, and there was talk of rebellion in the air. Paterson had learned to be a very good speaker at Princeton and had practiced his skills in the years since he had graduated.

He also seemed to have developed some very strange views. In 1773 he published a pamphlet arguing that doctors of the state were deliberately going around spreading smallpox. In those days smallpox was a very serious disease, and the charge was a serious one and apparently based on no real evidence. Paterson's career was a great one, but that does not change the fact that he was a pretty odd character.

As the year 1775 came, and with it the battles in Lexington and Concord, Paterson put his skills to work. When word of the British-American clashes reached New Jersey, a provincial congress was called to discuss what reaction New Jersey might take to the events in Massachusetts. Paterson was selected to be a delegate to that congress.

The governor of New Jersey was William Franklin, the son of Benjamin Franklin. Governor Franklin was loyal to the king who had appointed him. He and the provincial congress saw things quite differently. But the congress had the support of the people and the governor only had the support of the king, who lived rather far away. The congress gradually took over most of the powers of the state. When the governor would not go along with the congress's decisions, he was ordered confined to his house. When he defied that order, he was sent off to be held a prisoner in Connecticut.

The provincial congress met to draft a new constitution for New Jersey. It is a sign of the reluctance of the colonists to break from Great Britain that the draft constitution contained an "escape clause." It said that the constitution would be void if the colonies and Great Britain settled their differences. In a way, the idea makes sense. The only way that the British and Americans would be able to settle their differences was if the British agreed to greater freedom for the colonists. They would not agree to self-government because that was the most that they could give up. If they agreed to something less than self-government then the New Jersey constitution would, in fact, be void because it was based on the idea of self-government.

Paterson opposed the new constitution because of this clause. He believed that the new constitution should provide for a complete break from the past; that there was no turning back from the war for independence. This was a fairly radical position for the time, and Paterson won his argument.

Shortly after the debate about the new constitution, Paterson was appointed to be the attorney general of New Jersey. For someone who had not managed to have any real success as a lawyer, this was a high honor. The next year, 1777, he was given the additional job of being a member of the Council of Safety. This was a special group, created by the legislature, to run the state during the war. The legislature recognized that it was not well suited to run a state in the middle of a war. And New Jersey was literally in the middle of the war. Much of the Revolution was fought between New York and Pennsylvania. The only thing between New York and Pennsylvania is New Jersey. That small state bore the brunt of the battle, and it was no place to have the government run by an assembly of fifty or more legislators.

In a short time Paterson went from being a struggling lawyer and storekeeper to holding three important state jobs at once—member of the Council of Safety, attorney general, and member of the provincial congress. Despite these many duties, he took time out in 1779 to marry Cornelia Bell. In 1780 their first daughter was born. His new family and his responsibilities to his state caused him to twice turn down a seat in the national Congress.

But as the war ended in 1783, tragedy struck Paterson's life. A second child died while still an infant, and Paterson's wife, Cornelia, weakened by the tragedy, died shortly after in childbirth. He married again the next year. This time his wife was Euphemia White, an old family friend.

Between the end of the war and the Constitutional Convention, Paterson increased his reputation as a lawyer and as a politician. When the time came to select delegates from New Jersey to attend the Convention, Paterson was an obvious choice.

Paterson made an immediate impact on at least one other delegate. William Pierce of Georgia recorded his impressions of each delegate. Of Paterson he said, "one of those men whose powers break in on you and create astonishment . . . of a disposition so favorable to his advancement that everyone seemed ready to exalt him with their praises." By the end of the Convention, there were certainly some delegates who wished that Paterson had stayed at home.

The small states could go along with most of the Virginia Plan. True, it was hard to say whether there should be one president or an executive committee. In any event, if an executive committee would be bad, it would be equally bad for both small states and large states. What really bothered the small states was the question of representation in the legislature.

The small states had a problem in presenting their case. When the vote on the Virginia Plan was to come up, Rhode Island was not represented (because it had decided not to send a delegation) and the delegates from New Hampshire had not yet arrived. That meant that the small states did not have as many votes as they hoped for. So, while they could not agree with the Virginia Plan, they would have to come up with some plan that would make the large states happy too.

Either the large states would control the government (through representation based on population) or the small states would have power in the government beyond their size (through a one-state-one-vote plan). It is fair to say that the question of a national government for the newly freed colonies hung in the balance on this difficult question. And the delegates knew it.

After the Virginia Plan had been presented and approved of in a general way, Paterson spoke and asked the Convention to wait for a while for the vote on the representation question. On Friday, June 8, they agreed to hold the vote on Monday, June 11. The weekend promised to be busy.

There were two choices: each side—large states and small—could hold firm to their positions and see who won in the showdown vote, or they could try to agree on a compromise. Through Monday's vote they would both test the waters a little. They would find out what their real strength was, how many votes they had. If the tally was close, either side would have to consider compromise because this was a united nation they were trying to create, not an empire.

Over the weekend Paterson met with Roger Sherman, of Connecticut, to work out a plan for Monday's vote. When Monday came, Sherman proposed a compromise— in one house of Congress each state would have one vote, in the other representation would be decided by population. But it was too soon to compromise. The large states knew that they could win the vote, and they did. By a vote of nine states to two it was decided that the lower house (what we now call the House of Representatives) would be a proportional body. By a vote of six to five it was concluded that the upper house (the Senate) would also be proportional.

Things were close though. These votes were just sample votes. They did not bind the convention. At least one small state, New Hampshire, was certain to send a delegation soon. That would force a tie vote. Even if New Hampshire never showed up, there were some cards Paterson could play that might change one vote or more. He was ready to play those cards.

Paterson was in a very difficult position. He came from New Jersey. Caught between New York and Pennsylvania,

New Jersey had no real port of its own. It was, and is, a highway between the major cities of Philadelphia and New York. No state had a greater interest in establishing a national government than did New Jersey. A strong national government meant that New Jersey would not be bullied by its neighbors. At the same time, it would do New Jersey very little good if a national government was established and its neighboring states, which were large, had complete control of it.

New Jersey had every reason to compromise, but Paterson could not let his neighbors know that this was true. If they did, then they would wait for New Jersey to make the first move. Each side had something to gain, but the first one to move might lose because the other side would think it weak. A very delicate game was involved, and Paterson's place in history is assured by the fact that he played the game very well.

The first thing that he needed to do was to show that he was serious. The next thing he needed to do was to develop and present a plan that was reasonable, but that caused the large states to worry. If he did those two things, then the large states would say to themselves, "Paterson is not fooling around here, and he has this plan that just might do us some harm. Maybe we had better talk to him."

On Friday, June 15, Paterson presented what became known as the New Jersey Plan. It was a tricky piece of work, for Paterson had thrown into it not only equal representation, but also a few items that had been rejected in the Virginia Plan but that had some support among the delegates. His plan had a committee run the executive branch instead of a president. It had a unicameral (one house) legislature. There were no national courts other than the Supreme Court.

Paterson may not have believed in all of these things, but he had created a package that might have some support. Those delegates who liked the idea of a committee running the government might care more about that than an issue such as equal representation. Paterson was trying to put a sugar coating on equal state representation.

All of this maneuvering might not have worried the large states too much. They were good debaters. They would point out to the convention that the New Jersey Plan was wrong (from their point of view) on the big issue—representation. They could argue the merits on each of the smaller points. But Paterson had included something else in the New Jersey Plan, something that showed he was playing for keeps and that stood a strong chance of disrupting the whole Convention. Paterson's plan was not written as a new Constitution to govern a new type of nation. It was written, instead, as a set of amendments to the Articles of Confederation.

As we know, a good argument could be made that the Convention had no right to do anything but propose amendments to the Articles. The Virginia Plan violated the bill Congress had passed to create a Convention to propose those amendments, and many of the delegates were bound by their state governments to do no more.

The New Jersey Plan threatened to bring this whole issue to a boil, and it was a very dangerous issue. If the delegates took it seriously enough, the Convention might have to recess while the delegates went back to their legislatures and the Congress. All of the agreements and all of the movement that had been generated would disappear.

On Tuesday, June 19, the New Jersey Plan came up for a vote. Hamilton and Madison opposed it vigorously. They made clear to the delegates their view that the plan was no more than a sham; a wolf in sheep's clothing. The wolf was equal representation, an idea already rejected by the Convention.

Hamilton and Madison carried the day. The New Jersey Plan was defeated, but the defeat was a costly one for the large states. The small states had nearly half the votes at the Convention. At a revote at the end of the Convention these small-state voters might combine with those delegates who felt that the only proper purpose of the Convention was to amend the Articles of Confederation. Such a union might reject any constitution at all. While no one from the large states was talking about a compromise, many of them must have known that a compromise would be necessary.

CHAPTER
5

Compromise
and Conclusion

The first month of the Convention had been marked by the strong voicing of intelligent plans. The people who offered these plans were bright and skillful and very young. In the last and most important phase of the Convention's work two older hands would take over. They were Roger Sherman, of Connecticut, and Benjamin Franklin, of Pennsylvania.

The Convention and the nation hung in the balance. Anything could happen. The delegates could become stubborn and not listen to each others' real concerns or they could abandon their care for important issues and let the popular feelings of the day take charge. Either course would have been relatively easy. But neither was followed. Instead, they chose the far more difficult path of listening to each other and working hard to adjust their own plans for the nation to take into account the legitimate concerns of others. This was not politics but statesmanship.

Anyone can be an ordinary politician. All that it takes is a fairly loud voice and a willingness to push for the interests of a few over the broader interests of a large number of people. One of the blessings of democracy is that many politicians become statesmen. They finally put aside the small issues and look at the large ones. Usually they do this when they are older and have seen more of the world and understand its needs. Some great leaders understand the world at a young age. But, for the most part, wisdom comes with age. That does not mean that young people are not intelligent or do not contribute great things to society. There are too many good examples of such people to ignore. But wisdom, a sense of what is right in the long term, often takes time to acquire.

In those June days, when the Convention was so bitterly divided, one elder statesman came forward to press for compromise. A few weeks later, at the end of the Convention, the oldest member of the Convention would speak at a crucial moment to urge the delegates in their final votes to put local interests aside.

The lives of Roger Sherman and Benjamin Franklin had much in common. Though Franklin was by far the better known of the two, Sherman had led a distinguished life and was a very important person in the new nation. John Adams described him as "one of the most sensible men in the world." Thomas Jefferson said he was "a man who never said a foolish thing in his life."

Sherman was born in Newton, Massachusetts, in April of 1721. His family had come to America from England in 1634 and they had not become very wealthy. His father

Roger Sherman was the elder statesman from Connecticut and had a reputation for fairness and common sense.

made his living by repairing shoes and working a small farm. Young Roger had very little education, though he could read and write, which was more than many poor children could do. He could also repair shoes.

Sherman's father died when he was still a teen-ager, and Roger had to go to work as a shoemaker to help out his young brothers and sisters. Two years later he moved the family to New Milford, Connecticut. The legend is that the family went by wagon while Roger walked the 100 miles.

In Connecticut he studied surveying on his own. George Washington, you may remember, was also a surveyor. A new and quickly growing nation needed many surveyors. When estates were measured in miles, not mere acres, and there were no cars to travel those miles quickly, every surveying job took a long time to complete and every large piece of property eventually needed a survey done to mark the legal boundaries of the land. Surveying required strong abilities in math, which were not common in colonial America.

Sherman did not become rich from his work, but he did earn enough to educate the younger children, and by 1749 he had enough money to get married. His first wife was Elizabeth Hartwell. Though she only lived eleven years longer, they had seven children. Sherman was married again a few years after her death to Elizabeth Prescott. This second marriage produced eight more children. The Sherman house must have been a full and lively one.

It is often the case that surveys are not done until there is some dispute about boundary lines. Thus Sherman was often hired as part of the preparation for a law suit. He enjoyed his contact with the law and began to study it on his own. In 1754, at the age of thirty-three, he was admitted to the bar in Connecticut.

Sherman started slowly in life compared to someone like Edmund Randolph. But once he became a lawyer his rise was spectacular. The next year he was elected to the legislature in Connecticut. Four years later he became a judge. By 1766, he was a judge, a member of the Governor's Council (the upper house of the legislature), and the treasurer of Yale College. In 1774, he began a twenty-year career in Congress.

Sherman and Benjamin Franklin are different from all the other people we have talked about. All of the others either were from wealthy families or had been very well educated, or both. Sherman and Franklin had neither advantage. Perhaps they succeeded because, when they were young, very few people in the colonies had either money or education. Perhaps the lack of both made them work all the harder.

Sherman was in Congress when the Declaration of Independence was approved. In fact, he was a member of the committee that drafted that document. He was also a member of the committee that drafted the Articles of Confederation and, as we know, he was a delegate to the Constitutional Convention. That made him a drafter and signer of the three most important documents in American history. No one else shares that honor.

Sherman was in his mid-fifties when the Revolution began. He did not serve in the army but kept his state offices, adding service on the Connecticut Committee of Safety, similar to the one that William Paterson served on in New Jersey. When the war ended, Sherman added yet another title, the mayor of New Haven, a job he kept for the rest of his life.

When it came time to choose the Connecticut delegation to the Convention, the name of Roger Sherman was a natural choice. He was among the most experienced politicians in the state, and he had a reputation for fairness and common sense that was unmatched by anyone in the colonies, with the possible exception of Benjamin Franklin.

It was natural, then, that when the Convention seemed to have reached a deadlock, someone like Roger Sherman would come forward. When the New Jersey Plan was on the floor for a vote, Sherman was among its strongest supporters. After it was defeated, he did not abandon the effort to try to reach a reasonable compromise. The small states had made their point by surrounding the main issue, representation, with other issues that might be attractive to some delegates.

Two weeks later the question came up again because the entire Virginia Plan was being reconsidered line by line. Equality of representation in the lower house was defeated again. But, when the votes were counted on the question of equal representation in the upper house, the result was a tie.

Now things were really difficult. No plan could win. No plan had a majority of states on its side. For five days the Convention simply stopped.

On July 2 the Convention resumed and it was decided

that a grand committee would be formed. The committee would have one member from each state and would try to work out a compromise acceptable to all. Perhaps it was because it was close to Independence Day, but it took the committee only three days to agree to a proposal prepared by Roger Sherman. This eventually became known as the Connecticut Compromise or the Great Compromise.

The plan was relatively simple. The large states would get proportional representation in the House of Representatives and the small states would get equal representation in the Senate. The concerns of the large states were smoothed over by requiring that all legislation dealing with money had to start in the House of Representatives. The Senate could not consider a tax or budget bill until the House had already done so.

Edmund Randolph had originally objected to the plan, on behalf of the large states. He argued that if one house was to have equal representation, then its powers should be sharply limited. This would create a system very much like the English system today in which the upper house, the House of Lords, has limited power. William Paterson countered by saying that if that was the view of the large states, they should all go home. The final decision was a compromise between those two views.

The large states asked for a one-day recess, during which they met and agreed that there was no sense in going it on their own.

Some of the Southern states were still not satisfied, since they wanted representation in the House to be on the basis of wealth, not population. Their reason for this was that there were millions of slaves in the South who were not regarded as people but as property. Thus these states would have more votes in Congress if their property was added up than they would if their people, not counting slaves, were added up.

To meet these concerns, James Wilson, of Pennsylvania, proposed that each slave be counted as three-fifths of a person for purposes of determining representation in the House of Representatives. This concept, so strange to people today, was accepted as a reasonable compromise and the grand committee reported its results to the Convention. While there was still much debate about the question of equal representation in the Senate, the large states could not win. On July 16 the crucial vote was taken. New York was not represented. Its delegates had gone home for a while on July 10. New Hampshire's delegation had not shown up yet because of lack of money, and Rhode Island never got around to sending a delegation.

Five states voted for equal representation in the Senate. These were New Jersey, Delaware, Connecticut, Maryland, and North Carolina. Virginia voted for proportional representation as did Pennsylvania, Georgia, and South Carolina. If Massachusetts went with the large states, there would be another tie. But the tie was in the Massachusetts delegation itself. Neither plan had a majority in that delegation and as a result it could not cast its vote. The Connecticut Compromise was approved by a five-to-four margin. The later arrival of New Hampshire would make this majority a safe one.

The Connecticut Compromise was one of the great moments in American history. Each side had a strong argument. The small states could argue that equal representation had always been the rule in America. The large states could argue that proportional representation was the only fair way to proceed. That neither side got what it wanted in the final vote is true. It is equally true, though, that both sides accepted the decision of the Convention.

There were other issues in the Convention and there were other compromises. The question of slavery came up again and again. We have seen how it arose in terms of representation. There was also a move to ban the importation of new slaves. While the overwhelming majority of slaves were in the South, that proposal had some Southern support. Virginia had more slaves than it needed. The price of slaves was dropping and the cost of keeping slaves was rising. The final document allowed the Congress to ban further importation of slaves after 1808. Even that modest limitation on slavery carried a price with it. In return for the slavery limitations, the South won the right to have the new national capital in its part of the country.

There were a great many details to cover. As you can see from the finished document (Appendix B), the Constitution contains many small provisions. It does not just speak in broad terms. It often gets right down to the smallest factors. On July 26, the Convention turned the whole document over to a committee on detail, which was to work out the less significant problems. Edmund Randolph did much of the writing for that committee. It completed its work in ten days. The entire month of August was spent going over these details item by item.

When that work was finished, another committee was created, the committee on style. It was this group's task to polish the language of the Constitution and to make sure that one provision was not inconsistent with another. That committee was chaired by William Johnson and included such people as James Madison and Alexander Hamilton. Most of the actual writing, though, seems to have been done by Gouverneur Morris. It finished its work in the astonishing time of two days.

It seemed fairly certain that the final draft would be approved by the members of the Convention itself. But more than their approval was required. The delegates had to leave Philadelphia and go back to Congress and their home states and fight for local ratification. A majority of the states had to approve the document before the Constitution would take effect. In order to overcome this final barrier, the delegates themselves would have to act as enthusiastic salesmen.

Reluctantly accepting a compromise is one thing, fighting for that compromise against people who are your friends and who are unhappy about what you have voted for is another thing entirely. The delegates needed to be sent off with confidence in what they had done and a commitment to work hard to see the job through. Once again an older hand was needed. This time it was Benjamin Franklin.

Franklin was born in Boston in 1706. At eighty-one, he was the oldest member of the Convention. Like Roger Sherman, he had been born into a family with neither money nor education. Indeed, as the youngest of seventeen children, Franklin had to find his own place in life without much help from his family.

His father, Josiah Franklin, was a soap- and candle-maker who had come from England in 1683. Young Ben left school at age ten to help out in his father's shop. Two years later he became an apprentice in the printing shop of his brother, James. James was both a printer and a newspaper publisher, and young Ben would slip articles signed with a false name under the door of the printshop. For a while, at age sixteen, he even edited the paper while his brother was in jail for printing articles critical of the colonial government.

But James had a strong temper and beat Ben and the other apprentices when they did something he didn't like. In his seventeenth year Ben had had enough. He sold his books and traveled to New York looking for work. Finding none and being short of money, he set off by foot to Philadelphia. There he found work with a printer and settled in.

He soon caught the eye of the colonial governor of Pennsylvania, William Keith. Keith urged him to go to London to purchase equipment for a printshop of his own and promised him financial backing. Franklin went to London in 1725, but Keith's promises proved to be empty. To support himself, Ben found work with a printer and stayed in London for a year and a half. Returning to Philadelphia, he saved money for two years and finally opened up his own printing business. Around the same time he founded a discussion group that was to become the American Philosophical Society and whose library was to become

A portrait of Benjamin Franklin as he would have looked a few years before the Convention.

the first circulating library in America. A circulating library is one that lends out books for members to take home and read.

He and his partner, Hugh Meredith, founded a newspaper, *The Pennsylvania Gazette.* It was widely read and its influence led to Franklin's receiving the contract to print money for Pennsylvania. Franklin had a wife, Deborah Read, and two children. We have already seen something of his son, William Franklin, the governor of New Jersey who remained loyal to the crown during the Revolution. While Franklin had many virtues, no one would ever claim that he was a good family man. He spent years abroad, and while he was home he was not noted for paying much attention to those closest to him.

In 1733, he published the first of twenty-five editions of *Poor Richard's Almanac.* This book of weather and farming information was also filled with proverbs Franklin invented for the occasion. Each year the book was a best seller, and Franklin would have been famous had he done nothing else in his life. But he did many other things.

He held several minor political positions, many of them dealing with postal matters, at which Franklin became an expert. His scientific efforts included the famous kite experiment designed to discover whether lightning was made up of electricity. He invented bifocal glasses and a useful stove to heat colonial houses.

His accomplishments were so widely respected that in 1754 he received honorary degrees from both Harvard and Yale. But Franklin's career was just beginning. In 1757, he was asked to represent the interests of the colony of Pennsylvania in London. This was the first of the diplomatic efforts that were really his greatest achievements. He spent five years at this post and was able to convince Parliament to reduce the taxes paid by the proprietors of Pennsylvania, the family of William Penn. At the conclusion of this effort he was awarded an honorary degree by Oxford University in England, as well. By this time Franklin was probably the best-known American in the world. While some others might be held in higher esteem in America, no American had Franklin's reputation in Europe.

He returned to America in 1762 to tour all of the colonies with the hope of improving the postal system, returning to London soon after to represent several colonies. He fought unsuccessfully against the Stamp Act and then sought to have the contract for printing the stamps placed with his printshop in Philadelphia. This brought a hostile reaction in the colonies. When he learned of this, he devoted his efforts to convincing Parliament to repeal the act. When that goal was reached, his popularity in America was regained.

He stayed in London until 1775, when he returned to become a member of the Continental Congress, the oldest member of that group even then. He was also made a member of the committee assigned to draft the Declaration of Independence. While Thomas Jefferson was the main author of that document, Franklin made many contributions, including one that had nothing to do with the actual writing.

After the committee delivered its draft to the Congress,

a number of changes were made. These changes upset Jefferson greatly. Franklin told him the story of a hat maker who put up in front of his shop a sign that read "John Thompson, Hatter, makes and sells hats for ready money." One person criticized the sign because, he said, it was obvious that someone who makes hats is a hatter and so that word was not needed. Another thought it unnecessary to say that Thompson made hats since the customers would not care who made the hats. A third person thought that the mention of "ready money" was not needed since it was obvious from the fact that hats were being sold. Yet another friend thought that all he really needed was a sign with a picture of a hat, since he clearly was not in business to give hats away and no one would really care what his name was.

Jefferson may not have appreciated the story, but the new nation appreciated Franklin's abilities as a diplomat. He returned to Europe, this time to France to represent all of the colonies. He was able to convince the French to aid them in their fight against Great Britain. With French help, the British were defeated in 1783, and Franklin helped negotiate the peace treaty.

He returned to America in 1785 to accept the post of president of the State of Pennsylvania, and two years later was chosen to be a delegate to the Convention being held in Philadelphia. Franklin spoke in many of the debates during the Convention. Often he needed help or asked someone to read his speech for him. It was clear during the Convention that there were a number of things about the Constitution Franklin did not like. His opposition would have been fatal to the efforts to have Congress and the states ratify it.

Those delegates who favored the Constitution must have been a little worried, then, when Franklin announced that he wished to speak on the last day of the Convention. The document itself had been approved by a majority of states and this day was to be the day that delegates signed the final copy. If Franklin refused to sign, many others might hesitate.

Franklin felt too weak to stand and read his speech so he handed it to his fellow Pennsylvanian, James Wilson. He began by stating that at one point in his life he had believed that he was always right. As he grew older he recognized that that was not the case. He noted that there were several parts of the document he disagreed with:

> I agree to this Constitution, with all its faults, if they are such; because I think a General Government is necessary for us. . . . I doubt, too, whether any other Convention we can obtain may be able to make a better Constitution. . . . Thus I consent, sir, to this Constitution, because I expect no better, and because I am not sure that it is not the best. The opinion I have had of its errors I sacrifice to the public good. I have never whispered a syllable of them. Within these walls they were born, and here they shall die. . . . On the whole, sir, I cannot help expressing a wish that every member of the Convention who may still have objections to it, would with me, on this occasion, doubt a little of his own infallibility. . . .

The Convention was deeply moved by Franklin's practical wisdom. In the end, though, three delegates did refuse to sign the document. They were Elbridge Gerry, of Massachusetts, George Mason, of Virginia, and another Virginian—Edmund Randolph, the man who had done as much as anyone to move the Convention along the path of national government it finally chose.

Franklin's words had helped many doubters, but it was clear that there was going to be a battle ahead. There was to be a very big battle indeed.

CHAPTER

6

Ratification

Benjamin Franklin's warm and wise words sent the Constitution off to the country to be debated. But the drafters had rather cleverly set the limits of debate. Article VII of the draft stated that the Constitution would be ratified when nine states had approved of it in conventions of their own. The Congress did not have to approve and the legislatures in the various states did not have to approve.

When you consider that the Convention's only authority was to propose to Congress changes in the Articles of Confederation, this provision was very odd. Who were they to bypass the Congress and the elected legislatures of the states? Who gave them the right to say that, when nine states approved, a new nation would be formed?

No one gave them these rights. They took them, boldly and without much debate. In many ways, the nation was ready for the Constitution. Not all people favored it, as we shall soon see. But most average Americans knew that their government was not working and wanted a change. The fact that living legends such as Washington and Franklin approved of this new plan made most people feel comfortable about it.

Those who were not happy with the new Constitution were unhappy for many different reasons. Some remembered that they had just fought a war to be free from the rule of a king and feared that the new government would become just another monarchy. They did not like the fact that there was a single president and that he could be reelected for as long as he lived. They recalled that Julius Caesar had turned down the crown of a king in Rome only to live as an emperor in fact.

Others had fears about the possibility of a standing army. In the late 1700s this was a very important issue. In fact, the United States had no real standing army until well into the twentieth century. The worry was that a standing army would allow the government to stay in power by force. To us, today, such fears seem groundless. We have a standing army; that is, we do not create an army to fight a war but, instead, always have an army in existence in case of trouble and the army has never, in this country, been used by a leader to stay in power.

Another group of opponents was concerned about money. They were merchants and farmers who had owed money to the British before the war. They had won the war and now wanted to make sure that they were not forced to pay their debts to the "enemy."

Slavery also divided the nation, as it was to do for another eighty years. Many felt that the compromise of ending the slave trade in twenty years was shameful. Others felt that it was a violation of their right to own slaves.

Any sane person looking at the situation might have packed up his bags and gone home. But the Federalists (supporters of the Constitution) had two big advantages over the anti-Federalists (opponents of the Constitution).

First, they were united and their opponents were not. The Federalists had one plan, the Constitution. The anti-Federalists had no plan. They could not stand up and defend the Articles of Confederation. No one believed that that document would work any better in the future than it had in the past. All they could do was say that they did not like the Constitution. When challenged they could not offer an alternative.

Second, time was against them. The ratification process would take less than a year because the Federalists were pushing hard to move it along as quickly as possible. The great majority of delegates to the Convention supported the Constitution, and they were people of great importance and power in their own states. Given the times, the difficulty in traveling from place to place, the need for special elections in each state to elect members of the state conventions, the time needed for debate, and the fact that the two largest states decided to sit back and wait for the others to act, the speed of the ratification process was incredible.

It all began in Pennsylvania, even before the Continental Congress had had a chance to consider the Constitution.

The Pennsylvania state legislature was due to adjourn only ten days after the Convention ended and in that time it had to approve of a ratification convention. The Pennsylvania delegates moved as quickly as they could, but the issue did not come up until the last day, September 28.

The vote on the question was set for 4:00 P.M. The anti-Federalists knew that they did not have a majority, but they also knew that if all of their members were absent, the legislature would lack a quorum. A *quorum* is the number of members who must be present in order for the legislature to take action. Normally a quorum is not hard to obtain since it usually involves only one-third or one-fourth of the members. But late in a session many members may have left for home. If then a group walks off, even though the group is a minority of the whole legislature, it can destroy the quorum.

The anti-Federalists left the legislature and went to a nearby inn, where they locked themselves in a room. But the Federalists were not going to be defeated. Early the next morning, a mob of Federalists broke into the room and carried two anti-Federalists to the legislature. That was enough to make a quorum. The vote in favor of holding a ratification convention to meet in late November was forty-five to two. This was a very poor way to begin a democracy.

In the meantime, the draft constitution had been sent to Congress. As we know, the convention had not included Congress in the ratification process. But approval by Congress was important. One of the main arguments against the Constitution was sure to be that the Convention had no right to propose a new constitution. Its job was to propose amendments to the Articles of Confederation. If Congress gave its approval to the work done in Philadelphia, this argument would lose some of its sting. Also, the members of Congress were, of course, people of importance in their home states. Their approval would add strength to the Federalists' cause.

Congress debated the question for eight days, not really a very long time. In the end, the decision was unanimous. Congress would send the "report" of the Convention to the states for their consideration. Congress was not really putting its stamp of approval on the Constitution. Its actions were more like throwing a hot potato over to the states.

October and November were quiet periods in the ratification process. It would take time for the states to approve their conventions, elect delegates, and gather together to debate. But the Federalists were busy.

In October, the first of a series of letters appeared in New York newspapers. It was signed "Publius." In those days it was very common for important people to write letters to the newspapers using some type of false name, such as "A Connecticut Farmer," "A Son of New Jersey," and other names. The name chosen might actually describe the writer, or it might be chosen to appeal to some group of readers, or to show learning. Latin names were popular. Using Latin showed that you were educated and the word used could carry a message. *Publius* comes from the Latin word that means "people." By signing the letter *Publius* the writer was suggesting that he spoke for the people.

In fact Publius was three people: Alexander Hamilton, James Madison, and John Jay. James Madison we have already met. Alexander Hamilton and John Jay were New York lawyers. Hamilton was very well known across the country because he had been one of George Washington's aides during the Revolution. Jay was not as well known, though he had played an important role in the Revolution, as well. He had served as the Ambassador to Spain during the latter part of the Revolution and had been one of the three Americans who worked out the treaty of peace with the British. Hamilton and Jay were to work together with James Madison on one of the most important books about government in American history: *The Federalist Papers*. The letters to newspapers these men wrote would form the basis of the book.

Even though Hamilton and Jay will have their names linked together forever because of *The Federalist Papers*, they came from very different backgrounds.

Alexander Hamilton was born on January 11, 1755, on the island of Nevis in the Caribbean. His father was a Scottish adventurer (a fancy word for someone who doesn't have a job but is unemployed in an interesting place) and his mother a somewhat mysterious Frenchwoman. Though his father was not very interested in working himself, he sent young Alexander off to work in an office at the age of eleven.

Apparently Alexander made an impression on those he worked with. When he was seventeen, his fellow employees collected enough money to send him to school at King's College (the early name of Columbia University) in New York. When the Revolution started, Hamilton quit college to join Washington's army. He served well, and Washington soon asked him to be one of his chief aides.

Hamilton's new job brought him into contact with some of the most important people in the colonies. Among these was General Philip Schuyler. Schuyler was a very wealthy

Alexander Hamilton had been one of Washington's aides during the revolution and was one of New York's delegates to the Constitutional Convention.

man and an important figure in the government of New York. In 1780 Hamilton married Schuyler's daughter, Elizabeth. The marriage made him wealthy and opened the doors to a career in politics.

Hamilton was well suited to politics. He was very smart. With the exception of Thomas Jefferson, who stood alone, Hamilton ranked among the very brightest of the founders of the new nation. He was an excellent writer. In addition to his Publius letters, he wrote a number of articles and pamphlets on government and was one of the first people to urge that the Articles of Confederation be abandoned in favor of a strong national government.

It was natural, then, that he would be chosen as one of New York's delegates to the Constitutional Convention. Hamilton voted in favor of the final document, but, in fact, he had serious questions about it. He felt that it gave too much power to the states and not enough power to the national government.

John Jay was not actually born with a silver spoon in his mouth, but he came from a very well-connected family. He was the eighth child of Peter Van Cortland Jay and his wife Mary. Van Cortland remains a famous name in New York City, where John was born. The name is also a sign of Jay's Dutch heritage and in the late 1700s, the Dutch were still very powerful in New York. His father was an important merchant and he had grand dreams for his children. He considered John to be the brightest of the large group and hoped that he would take up the religious life.

John Jay entered King's College in 1760, a dozen years

John Jay served his country well in a number of important positions, including his appointment as the first Chief Justice of the United States.

before Hamilton, at the age of fifteen. Instead of theology, he studied law and became a member of the bar in 1768. The next year he was appointed to settle a boundary dispute between New York and New Jersey and in that role showed great skill at negotiation. He practiced law in New York for a few years and did not involve himself much in the politics of the day. He married Sarah Livingston in 1774. She was the daughter of another famous New York family. The path ahead was easy for Jay. Wealth, political power, and influence with the government were guaranteed to him for the rest of his life.

In one sense he had nothing to rebel against. He, along with George Washington and Edmund Randolph and many other revolutionaries, had everything they could ever want. In fact, Jay was not very much in favor of revolution. He was a problem solver. He had a talent for bringing people together and listening to both sides and getting them to listen to each other. War would not appeal to such a man.

Nevertheless, Jay was elected to the first Continental Congress and even finally supported the Declaration of Independence. He then became chief justice of New York (while still in his early thirties) and, in 1778, was elected president of the Congress itself.

But Jay's natural skills as a diplomat were too strong to ignore. In 1779 the Congress asked him to go to Spain as the American ambassador. There were three important countries in Europe at the time: England, France, and Spain. America was at war with England. Benjamin Franklin was serving as ambassador to France. Jay's selection for Madrid showed how much his countrymen thought of him.

Jay was very good at his job. He kept the Spanish neutral. That wasn't too hard because the English and the Spanish had been fighting for centuries and the Spanish were nervous about their own colonies along the Mississippi River. But Jay also convinced the Spanish to allow the sale of gunpowder and artillery to the Americans. Since there was very little hope that the Spanish would ever be paid for their goods, this was a difficult job.

After Washington defeated the British at Yorktown, Jay joined Benjamin Franklin in Paris. There they were met by John Adams. Together the three negotiated the Treaty of Paris, which ended the war on terms very favorable to the Americans.

Jay returned home in 1784 and served as secretary of foreign affairs under the Articles of Confederation until Washington took over as president under the new constitution. Jay was not a member of the Constitutional Convention, but his experience in foreign affairs made him an expert on the failings of the Articles of Confederation in that area. So when Hamilton and Madison began to plan their series of articles under the name Publius, John Jay was the natural person to seek out when it came to questions about such matters.

There were eighty-five letters written by Publius and collected together as *The Federalist Papers.* Hamilton wrote fifty-one of them. Madison wrote twenty-six. Jay was the author of only five of the letters because he became ill in the middle of the project. Three letters were written jointly by Hamilton and Madison.

The letters cover virtually every aspect of government

and of the new Constitution. Each provides what lawyers would call a "brief" on one subject. For instance in *Federalist* 82 (the letters are always referred to by number, they have no titles), Hamilton wrote about the Supreme Court. The anti-Federalists were arguing that the Supreme Court established by the new Constitution would have the power to overrule state and local courts. This was a serious argument because it created a fear that the national government would be running the daily lives of the people from some remote capital. That would be no better than rule from London.

If a farmer claims that he owns a certain piece of property and someone else says that they own it instead, they may end up in court. A deed in those days might have said something like "Jones' property begins at the stump in the swamp and runs to the large boulder near Mary Smith's barn." A judge or jury deciding where the property line was might know that in that area *swamp* meant any place that was usually wet in spring, or that a *boulder* was any rock too heavy to pick up. Would nine Federal judges in Washington understand and approve these local common-sense rules, or would they give their own meaning to the words?

Hamilton pointed out that the Supreme Court would not be able to overrule local courts on local matters. Only questions of Federal law could be decided by the Supreme Court.

In *Federalist* 5, Jay wrote about a much broader argument against the Constitution. There were some who thought that the thirteen colonies were too far apart and too different from each other to be just one nation. They suggested that there should be four nations: New England, the Mid-Atlantic States, the South, and the West.

Again, this was a serious argument. The regions really did not have much in common with each other. Climate, commerce, religion, politics, attitudes about slavery, and mother countries divided them. The idea of four nations with some loose connection had a strong appeal.

Jay answered the argument by describing events in European history. European nations had been fighting each other for the better part of seven centuries. The idea of four nations in the New World would just create the same spirit of rivalry that had caused so much trouble in the Old World. In addition, four small nations would be weaker than one large nation in opposing attacks from foreign nations. The fear of such attacks was a real one, since France and Spain still held territory next to the original thirteen states.

One of the most interesting things about *The Federalist Papers* is that the letters always treat the arguments seriously. They do not say that the idea of four nations is ridiculous. They do not attack the honesty or intelligence of the persons presenting the argument. They treat their opponents with respect. This was very different from the rough-and-tumble, name-calling political style that was common in those days (and not unusual today).

It is not true that *The Federalist Papers* led to the approval of the Constitution. The real importance of the letters is that they were statements by important and thoughtful people of the late 1700s. Their view of what the Constitution meant was and is a significant one. Every year the Supreme Court of the United States and other courts will quote *The Federalist Papers* to show what the Constitution meant to people who helped to write it.

There is a saying, though, that "all politics is local." Local issues probably played the most important part in the ratification process. If people in North Carolina believed that the Constitution would be good for them, then they would approve it. They probably did not know anybody in Massachusetts or New York. Their basic concern was for their own state.

That does not mean that the issues were different in each state. Everyone was concerned about trade between the states and about the ability to raise taxes to pay for national needs. But there was a basic agreement about these and other issues that had caused the states to come to the Convention to begin with. The disagreements would not be on those issues. The Articles of Confederation had not worked, and no one was really opposed to making changes that would make them work. The problems would come in those areas where the Convention had gone past its instructions to amend the Articles.

In setting up an entirely new form of government, the Convention's delegates had created a whole new set of problems. No one really knew how the new government would work. One of the basic fears in life is the fear of the unknown. But everyone in America had faced the unknown when they or their forebears had come across the ocean to begin with or had faced life in a new and untamed land. Because of this history, Americans were probably more willing to try something new than most people would be.

At the start of the ratification effort, it seemed as though there would be no trouble at all. On December 7, 1787, Delaware's special convention approved the new Constitution unanimously. Of course Delaware, as a small state, felt it was getting a good deal. It had gained equality with the large states in the Senate and, in joining with the other states to form a new nation, it had protected itself in two ways. First, it was protected from foreign attack. On its own, it could have been taken by any nation in the world. Second, it had protected itself from economic attack by its large neighbors, especially Pennsylvania.

Delaware's approval was not surprising, but the next state to approve was Pennsylvania, one of the large states. Its convention met on November 30, 1787, and the debate was bitter. The anti-Federalists would not forget how they had been kidnapped on the day the legislature voted to hold the convention. James Wilson led the Federalist forces. For twelve days he stayed on the floor of the convention answering every argument. On December 12 the final vote came. The Constitution was approved by a vote of forty-six to twenty-three. Two weeks later the anti-Federalists had their revenge. A mob attacked and beat Wilson badly.

Four days later, the New Jersey convention voted unanimously in favor of the Constitution. Nine states were needed to make the Constitution official and three had approved within ten days of each other. But Christmas and winter were coming. The pace would slow, and when it slowed the Constitution would be in danger. The energy of the Federalists would be highest at the beginning and the anti-Federalists would not be well organized then. Both those situations could change by spring.

In January Georgia and Connecticut gave their approval. Neither vote was surprising. Connecticut had sponsored the compromise that made the Constitution possible. As a small state between New York and Massachusetts, it supported the Constitution for many of the same reasons that Delaware and New Jersey did. Georgia also had a strong reason for approving. Strange as it may seem to us today, in 1788 Georgia was the wildest part of the wild frontier. It was the only one of the states with a serious Indian war going on and the Spanish colonists in the "west" were threatening its borders. Georgia needed outside help, and the Constitution was one way to get it.

On January 9, 1788, the Massachusetts Convention began its sessions. Its meeting would last almost a month and would change the whole course of the ratification effort.

Massachusetts was where it had all begun. Real opposition to British rule began there. The Revolution began there. The effort to create a new Constitution began there, too. For it was in Massachusetts that Daniel Shays and the angry farmers who followed him had shown the real weaknesses of the new nation. Massachusetts was as divided in early 1788 as it had been at the height of Shays's Rebellion.

One of the three delegates at the Convention to vote against the Constitution was Elbridge Gerry, of Massachusetts. Gerry was not a delegate to the ratification convention. He had run for a seat in eastern Massachusetts, which was strong Federalist territory, and he had lost. But the anti-Federalists were a majority in the convention, thanks to strong representation from the western part of the state—Shays's territory.

While the anti-Federalists were a majority, they were poorly organized. Numbers do not guarantee a win if a minority has a clear goal in mind and the majority is split into several different groups.

The anti-Federalists were split into groups favoring farmers, groups opposing standing armies, and groups favoring a Bill of Rights. Before the Massachusetts convention began Samuel Adams, John Hancock and others got together and prepared nine amendments to the Constitution. These were designed to provide a Bill of Rights. The amendments were written as recommendations to the first Congress to meet under the Constitution.

That proposal knocked the breath out of the anti-Federalists. Many of them switched their votes because of it. One, William Symmes, of Andover, was forced out of town when he voted with the hated Federalists.

Massachusetts approved in late January by a vote of 187 to 168. That made the total six in favor of the Constitution, none opposed. Anyone would be happy with a six-to-nothing lead, but New York and Virginia had not voted yet. Without those two giants, there would be no union of the states.

In April, the state of Maryland gave its approval by a much wider margin (sixty-three to eleven). But Maryland also proposed amendments similar to those suggested by

Massachusetts. South Carolina followed Maryland in May. The pro-Constitution vote was strong there also (149 to 46). Only one more state was needed to create a new nation.

Three states were about to hold their conventions: New Hampshire, Virginia, and New York. North Carolina would hold its much later. The thirteenth state, Rhode Island and Providence Plantation, had not sent delegates to the Convention and was not planning to do anything about the Constitution. There was little reason to doubt that New Hampshire would approve. But the support of New York and Virginia was crucial. They had the largest populations and the most wealth in America. Each was a doorway to its region. Virginia controlled the commerce to the south and New York did the same to the north.

In Virginia the opposition was led by one important member of the Convention, George Mason, aided by one of the most famous debaters in American history, Patrick Henry.

In New York, the governor, George Clinton, led the fight against ratification. He was opposed by Hamilton and Jay. The New York convention was just getting started at Poughkeepsie when word came that New Hampshire had approved, though the vote was relatively close. Attention turned to Virginia.

The battle there had been as fierce as it had been anywhere. George Mason and Patrick Henry had counted on the help of Edmund Randolph in opposing ratification. Randolph, after all, had been one of only three delegates to the Philadelphia Convention who had not signed the final document. But Randolph disappointed them.

Instead of opposing ratification, he stood up at the convention in Richmond and stated that, if the states did not approve the Constitution, the rest of the world would look on them as a people who had been willing to fight for freedom but would not run a risk to keep it.

"I am a friend to the Union," he concluded, and with his support the Federalists carried the day by a vote of eighty-nine to seventy-nine. Of course, Randolph's language was not the only factor. Washington was not at the convention, but his giant figure loomed over all of its meetings. The much smaller figure of James Madison was at the convention but did not loom. He darted from place to place, answering every argument with great detail and great care.

The vote in Virginia came on June 25, 1788, just four days after the New Hampshire vote. Only New York, among the large states, remained to be heard from.

In New York, the delegates were strongly anti-Federalist. But even the most vocal opponent of the Constitution could not deny that the battle was really over. Ten states had ratified. Only New York, North Carolina, and Rhode Island had not been heard from. The Federalists felt strong enough to oppose a Bill of Rights as a condition of ratification. Hamilton attacked the idea at every point. Hamilton was a talented man but never a very popular one. His support of the Federalist cause may have done more harm than good. John Jay finally stepped in with a compromise.

The convention would not require a Bill of Rights to give its approval to the Constitution. Instead the delegates would sign a letter calling for a second Constitutional Convention to propose such a document. On July 26, New York ratified by a vote of thirty to twenty-seven.

The deed was done and done well. A new Constitution had been approved with a form of government unlike any that the world had ever seen. A new nation had been formed and the world stepped forward into the Age of Democracy.

AFTERWORD

The people whom we have seen in this book lived on after the Convention, of course. Some went on to greater things. Others would mark the Convention as the high point of their lives.

George Washington was unanimously selected as the first president of the United States of America. He served in that office for two terms and then retired once more to his beloved Mount Vernon, where he died on December 14, 1799, at the age of sixty-seven.

James Madison served in the House of Representatives from 1789 to 1797. From 1801 to 1809 he served as secretary of state in the cabinet of his friend, Thomas Jefferson. He was elected to follow Jefferson in the presidency and was reelected to serve a second term. When Jefferson died, Madison followed him again, this time as the head of the University of Virginia. He died at his home, Montpelier, on June 28, 1836.

Edmund Randolph was named by President Washington to be the first attorney general of the United States. He served in that office until 1794, when he took over from Thomas Jefferson as secretary of state. The next year a letter from the French ambassador to his superiors in Paris was discovered by the British, who turned it over to Washington. The letter suggested that Randolph had disclosed national secrets to the French and even that he had asked for money. The truth of the charges was never established, but Randolph resigned in disgrace. He returned to Virginia, where he died in 1813.

William Paterson was chosen to be one of New Jersey's first senators and thus joined the part of Congress in which each state was equally represented. He left the Senate to become governor of New Jersey. In 1793, George Washington nominated him to the Supreme Court of the United States. He was a useful, though not great, member of that court until his death in 1806.

Roger Sherman represented Connecticut in the House of Representatives (1789–91) and then the United States Senate (1791–93). He died in New Haven, Connecticut, on July 23, 1793.

Benjamin Franklin retired from his position as president of the Commonwealth of Pennsylvania in 1788. Though in poor health, he spent the next two years as president of the Society for Promoting the Abolition of Slavery. He died on April 17, 1790, at the age of eighty-four in the city of Philadelphia.

Alexander Hamilton was chosen by George Washington to be the first secretary of the treasury. His financial abilities allowed the United States to quickly establish itself as a power in world commerce. Hamilton left the cabinet in 1795 and practiced law in New York. He remained interested in politics, though, and worried that some politicians might not be as interested in the nation as they were in their own fortunes. He told other people that Jefferson's vice-president, Aaron Burr, was a dangerous and untrustworthy man. Burr challenged Hamilton to a duel. They met in Weehawken, New Jersey, on July 11, 1804. Hamilton had no wish to harm Burr and fired his shot in the air. Burr's bullet struck Hamilton, who died the next day.

John Jay was chosen by Washington to be the first chief justice of the United States Supreme Court. While holding that office, he went to London to negotiate a treaty with the British. On his return in 1795, he learned that he had been elected governor of New York. He held that position until 1801, when he retired. He died in 1829. Like Franklin, Jay was eighty-four at his death.

APPENDIX

A

Delegates to
the Constitutional
Convention

Connecticut

William Samuel Johnson
Roger Sherman
Oliver Ellsworth

Delaware

George Read
Gunning Bedford, Jr.
John Dickinson
Richard Bassett
Jacob Broom

Georgia

William Few
Abraham Baldwin
William Pierce
William Houstoun

Maryland

James McHenry
Daniel of St. Thomas Jenifer
Daniel Carroll
John Francis Mercer
Luther Martin

Massachusetts

Elbridge Gerry
Nathaniel Gorham
Rufus King
Caleb Strong

New Hampshire

John Langdon
Nicholas Gilman

New Jersey

David Brearley
William Churchill Houston
William Paterson
William Livingston
Jonathan Dayton

New York

Robert Yates
Alexander Hamilton
John Lansing, Jr.

North Carolina

Alexander Martin
William Richardson Davie
Richard Dobbs Spaight
William Blount
Hugh Williamson

Pennsylvania

Thomas Mifflin

Robert Morris
George Clymer
Jared Ingersoll
Thomas Fitzsimons
James Wilson
Gouverneur Morris
Benjamin Franklin

South Carolina

John Rutledge
Charles Pinckney
Charles Cotesworth Pinckney
Pierce Butler

Virginia

George Washington
Edmund Randolph
John Blair
James Madison, Jr.
George Mason
George Wythe
James McClurg

APPENDIX

B

The Constitution

of the

United States

of America

We the People of the United States, in Order to form a more perfect Union, establish Justice, insure domestic Tranquility, provide for the common defence, promote the general Welfare, and secure the Blessings of Liberty to ourselves and our Posterity, do ordain and establish this Constitution for the United States of America.

Article I

SECTION 1.   All legislative Powers herein granted shall be vested in a Congress of the United States, which shall consist of a Senate and House of Representatives.

SECTION 2.   The House of Representatives shall be composed of Members chosen every second Year by the People of the several States, and the Electors in each State shall have the Qualifications requisite for Electors of the most numerous Branch of the State Legislature.

No Person shall be a Representative who shall not have attained to the Age of twenty five Years, and been seven Years a Citizen of the United States, and who shall not, when elected, be an Inhabitant of that State in which he shall be chosen.

Representatives and direct Taxes shall be apportioned among the several States which may be included within this Union, according to their respective Numbers, which shall be determined by adding to the whole Number of free Persons, including those bound to Service for a Term of Years, and excluding Indians not taxed, three fifths of all other Persons. The actual Enumeration shall be made within three Years after the first Meeting of the Congress of the United States, and within every subsequent Term of ten Years, in such Manner as they shall by Law direct. The Number of Representatives shall not exceed one for every thirty Thousand, but each State shall have at Least one Representative; and until such enumeration shall be made, the State of New Hampshire shall be entitled to chuse three, Massachusetts eight, Rhode Island and Providence Plantations one, Connecticut five, New-York six, New Jersey four, Pennsylvania eight, Delaware one, Maryland six, Virginia ten, North Carolina five, South Carolina five, and Georgia three.

When vacancies happen in the Representation from any State, the Executive Authority thereof shall issue Writs of Election to fill such Vacancies.

The House of Representatives shall chuse their Speaker and other Officers; and shall have the sole Power of Impeachment.

SECTION 3. The Senate of the United States shall be composed of two Senators from each State, chosen by the

Legislature thereof, for six Years; and each Senator shall have one Vote.

Immediately after they shall be assembled in Consequence of the first Election, they shall be divided as equally as may be into three Classes. The Seats of the Senators of the first Class shall be vacated at the Expiration of the second Year, of the second Class at the Expiration of the fourth Year, and of the third Class at the Expiration of the sixth Year, so that one third may be chosen every second Year; and if Vacancies happen by Resignation, or otherwise, during the Recess of the Legislature of any State, the Executive thereof may make temporary Appointments until the next Meeting of the Legislature, which shall then fill such Vacancies.

No Person shall be a Senator who shall not have attained to the Age of thirty Years, and been nine Years a Citizen of the United States, and who shall not, when elected, be an Inhabitant of that State for which he shall be chosen.

The Vice President of the United States shall be President of the Senate, but shall have no Vote, unless they be equally divided.

The Senate shall chuse their other Officers, and also a President pro tempore, in the Absence of the Vice President, or when he shall exercise the Office of President of the United States.

The Senate shall have the sole Power to try all Impeachments. When sitting for that Purpose, they shall be on Oath or Affirmation. When the President of the United States is tried, the Chief Justice shall preside: And no Person shall be convicted without the Concurrence of two thirds of the Members present.

Judgment in Cases of Impeachment shall not extend further than to removal from Office, and disqualification to hold and enjoy any Office of honor, Trust or Profit under the United States: but the Party convicted shall nevertheless be liable and subject to Indictment, Trial, Judgment and Punishment, according to Law.

SECTION 4.   The Times, Places and Manner of holding Elections for Senators and Representatives, shall be prescribed in each State by the Legislature thereof; but the Congress may at any time by Law make or alter such Regulations, except as to the Places of chusing Senators.

The Congress shall assemble at least once in every Year, and such Meeting shall be on the first Monday in December, unless they shall by Law appoint a different Day.

SECTION 5.   Each House shall be the Judge of the Elections, Returns and Qualifications of its own Members, and a Majority of each shall constitute a Quorum to do Business; but a smaller Number may adjourn from day to day, and may be authorized to compel the Attendance of absent Members, in such Manner, and under such Penalties as each House may provide.

Each House may determine the Rules of its Proceedings, punish its Members for disorderly Behaviour, and, with the Concurrence of two thirds, expel a Member.

Each House shall keep a Journal of its Proceedings, and from time to time publish the same, excepting such Parts as may in their Judgment require Secrecy; and the Yeas and Nays of the Members of either House on any question shall, at the Desire of one fifth of those Present, be entered on the Journal.

Neither House, during the Session of Congress, shall, without the Consent of the other, adjourn for more than three days, nor to any other Place than that in which the two Houses shall be sitting.

SECTION 6. The Senators and Representatives shall receive a Compensation for their Services, to be ascertained by Law, and paid out of the Treasury of the United States. They shall in all Cases, except Treason, Felony and Breach of the Peace, be privileged from Arrest during their Attendance at the Session of their respective Houses, and in going to and returning from the same; and for any Speech or Debate in either House, they shall not be questioned in any other Place.

No Senator or Representative shall, during the Time for which he was elected, be appointed to any civil Office under the Authority of the United States, which shall have been created, or the Emoluments whereof shall have been encreased during such time; and no Person holding any Office under the United States, shall be a Member of either House during his Continuance in Office.

SECTION 7. All Bills for raising Revenue shall originate in the House of Representatives; but the Senate may propose or concur with Amendments as on other Bills.

Every Bill which shall have passed the House of Representatives and the Senate, shall, before it become a Law, be presented to the President of the United States; If he approve he shall sign it, but if not he shall return it, with his Objections to that House in which it shall have originated, who shall enter the Objections at large on their Journal, and proceed to reconsider it. If after such Reconsideration two thirds of that House shall agree to pass the Bill, it shall be sent, together with the Objections, to the other House, by which it shall likewise be reconsidered, and if approved by two thirds of that House, it shall become a Law. But in all such Cases the Votes of both Houses shall be determined by Yeas and Nays, and the Names of the Persons voting for and against the Bill shall be entered on the Journal of each House respectively. If any Bill shall not be returned by the President within ten Days (Sundays excepted) after it shall have been presented to him, the Same shall be a Law, in like Manner as if he had signed it, unless the Congress by their Adjournment prevent its Return, in which Case it shall not be a Law.

Every Order, Resolution, or Vote to which the Concurrence of the Senate and House of Representatives may be necessary (except on a question of Adjournment) shall be presented to the President of the United States; and before the Same shall take Effect, shall be approved by him, or being disapproved by him, shall be repassed by two thirds of the Senate and House of Representatives, according to the Rules and Limitations prescribed in the Case of a Bill.

SECTION 8.   The Congress shall have Power To lay and collect Taxes, Duties, Imposts and Excises, to pay the Debts and provide for the common Defence and general Welfare of the United States; but all Duties, Imposts and Excises shall be uniform throughout the United States;

To borrow Money on the credit of the United States;

To regulate Commerce with foreign Nations, and among the several States, and with the Indian Tribes;

To establish an uniform Rule of Naturalization, and uniform Laws on the subject of Bankruptcies throughout the United States;

To coin Money, regulate the Value thereof, and of foreign Coin, and fix the Standard of Weights and Measures;

To provide for the Punishment of counterfeiting the Securities and current Coin of the United States;

To establish Post Offices and post Roads;

To promote the Progress of Science and useful Arts, by securing for limited Times to Authors and Inventors the exclusive Right to their respective Writings and Discoveries;

To constitute Tribunals inferior to the supreme Court;

To define and punish Piracies and Felonies committed on the high Seas, and Offences against the Law of Nations;

To declare War, grant Letters of Marque and Reprisal, and make Rules concerning Captures on Land and Water;

To raise and support Armies, but no Appropriation of Money to that Use shall be for a longer Term than two Years;

To provide and maintain a Navy;

To make Rules for the Government and Regulation of the land and naval Forces;

To provide for calling forth the Militia to execute the Laws of the Union, suppress Insurrections and repel Invasions;

To provide for organizing, arming, and disciplining, the Militia, and for governing such Part of them as may be employed in the Service of the United States, reserving to the States respectively, the Appointment of the Officers, and the Authority of training the Militia according to the discipline prescribed by Congress;

To exercise exclusive Legislation in all Cases whatsoever, over such District (not exceeding ten Miles square) as may, by Cession of particular States, and the Acceptance of Congress, become the Seat of the Government of the United States, and to exercise like Authority over all Places purchased by the Consent of the Legislature of the State in which the Same shall be, for the Erection of Forts, Magazines, Arsenals, dock-Yards, and other needful Buildings;—And

To make all Laws which shall be necessary and proper for carrying into Execution the foregoing Powers, and all other Powers vested by this Constitution in the Government of the United States, or in any Department or Officer thereof.

SECTION 9.   The Migration or Importation of such Persons as any of the States now existing shall think proper to admit, shall not be prohibited by the Congress prior to the Year one thousand eight hundred and eight, but a Tax or duty may be imposed on such Importation, not exceeding ten dollars for each Person.

The Privilege of the Writ of Habeas Corpus shall not be suspended, unless when in Cases of Rebellion or Invasion the public Safety may require it.

No Bill of Attainder or ex post facto Law shall be passed.

No Capitation, or other direct, Tax shall be laid, unless in Proportion to the Census or Enumeration herein before directed to be taken.

No Tax or Duty shall be laid on Articles exported from any State.

No Preference shall be given by any Regulation of Commerce or Revenue to the Ports of one State over those of another:

nor shall Vessels bound to, or from, one State, be obliged to enter, clear, or pay Duties in another.

No Money shall be drawn from the Treasury, but in Consequence of Appropriations made by Law; and a regular Statement and Account of the Receipts and Expenditures of all public Money shall be published from time to time.

No Title of Nobility shall be granted by the United States: And no Person holding any Office of Profit or Trust under them, shall, without the Consent of the Congress, accept of any present, Emolument, Office, or Title, of any kind whatever, from any King, Prince, or foreign State.

SECTION 10.   No State shall enter into any Treaty, Alliance, or Confederation; grant Letters of Marque and Reprisal; coin Money; emit Bills of Credit; make any Thing but gold and silver Coin a Tender in Payment of Debts; pass any Bill of Attainder, ex post facto Law, or Law impairing the Obligation of Contracts, or grant any Title of Nobility.

No State shall, without the Consent of the Congress, lay any Imposts or Duties on Imports or Exports, except what may be absolutely necessary for executing its inspection Laws: and the net Produce of all Duties and Imposts, laid by any State on Imports or Exports, shall be for the Use of the Treasury of the United States; and all such Laws shall be subject to the Revision and Controul of the Congress.

No State shall, without the Consent of Congress, lay any Duty of Tonnage, keep Troops, or Ships of War in time of Peace, enter into any Agreement or Compact with another State, or with a foreign Power, or engage in War, unless actually invaded, or in such imminent Danger as will not admit of delay.

Article II

SECTION 1. The executive Power shall be vested in a President of the United States of America. He shall hold his Office during the Term of four Years, and, together with the Vice President, chosen for the same Term, be elected, as follows

Each State shall appoint, in such Manner as the Legislature thereof may direct, a Number of Electors, equal to the whole Number of Senators and Representatives to which the State may be entitled in the Congress: but no Senator or Representative, or Person holding an Office of Trust or Profit under the United States, shall be appointed an Elector.

The Electors shall meet in their respective States, and vote by Ballot for two Persons, of whom one at least shall not be an Inhabitant of the same State with themselves. And they shall make a List of all the Persons voted for, and of the Number of Votes for each; which List they shall sign and certify, and transmit sealed to the Seat of the Government of the United States, directed to the President of the Senate. The President of the Senate shall, in the Presence of the Senate and House of Representatives, open all the Certificates, and the Votes shall then be counted. The Person having the greatest Number of Votes shall be the President, if such Number be a Majority of the whole Number of Electors appointed; and if there be more than one who have such Majority, and have an equal Number of Votes, then the House of Representatives shall immediately chuse by Ballot one of them for President; and if no Person have a Majority, then from the five highest on the List the said House shall in like Manner chuse the President. But in chusing the President, the Votes shall be taken by States, the

Representation from each State having one Vote; A quorum for this Purpose shall consist of a Member or Members from two thirds of the States, and a Majority of all the States shall be necessary to a Choice. In every Case, after the Choice of the President, the Person having the greatest Number of Votes of the Electors shall be the Vice President. But if there should remain two or more who have equal Votes, the Senate shall chuse from them by Ballot the Vice President.

The Congress may determine the Time of chusing the Electors, and the Day on which they shall give their Votes; which Day shall be the same throughout the United States.

No Person except a natural born Citizen, or a Citizen of the United States, at the time of the Adoption of this Constitution, shall be eligible to the Office of President; neither shall any Person be eligible to that Office who shall not have attained to the Age of thirty five Years, and been fourteen Years a Resident within the United States.

In Case of the Removal of the President from Office, or of his Death, Resignation, or Inability to discharge the Powers and Duties of the said Office, the Same shall devolve on the Vice President, and the Congress may by Law provide for the Case of Removal, Death, Resignation or Inability, both of the President and Vice President, declaring what Officer shall then act as President, and such Officer shall act accordingly, until the Disability be removed, or a President shall be elected.

The President shall, at stated Times, receive for his Services, a Compensation, which shall neither be encreased nor diminished during the Period for which he shall have been elected, and he shall not receive within that Period any other Emolument from the United States, or any of them.

Before he enter on the Execution of his Office, he shall take the following Oath or Affirmation:—"I do solemnly swear (or affirm) that I will faithfully execute the Office of President of the United States, and will to the best of my Ability, preserve, protect and defend the Constitution of the United States."

SECTION 2.   The President shall be Commander in Chief of the Army and Navy of the United States, and of the Militia of the several States, when called into the actual Service of the United States; he may require the Opinion, in writing, of the principal Officer in each of the executive Departments, upon any Subject relating to the Duties of their respective Offices, and he shall have Power to grant Reprieves and Pardons for Offences against the United States, except in Cases of Impeachment.

He shall have Power, by and with the Advice and Consent of the Senate, to make Treaties, providing two thirds of the Senators present concur; and he shall nominate, and by and with the Advice and Consent of the Senate, shall appoint Ambassadors, other public Ministers and Consuls, Judges of the supreme Court, and all other Officers of the United States, whose Appointments are not herein otherwise provided for, and which shall be established by Law: but the Congress may by Law vest the Appointment of such inferior Officers, as they think proper, in the President alone, in the Courts of Law, or in the Heads of Departments.

The President shall have Power to fill up all Vacancies that may happen during the Recess of the Senate, by granting Commissions which shall expire at the End of their next Session.

SECTION 3.   He shall from time to time give to the Congress Information of the State of the Union, and recommend to their

Consideration such Measures as he shall judge necessary and expedient; he may, on extraordinary Occasions, convene both Houses, or either of them, and in Case of Disagreement between them, with Respect to the Time of Adjournment, he may adjourn them to such Time as he shall think proper; he shall receive Ambassadors and other public Ministers; he shall take Care that the Laws be faithfully executed, and shall Commission all the Officers of the United States.

SECTION 4.   The President, Vice President and all civil Officers of the United States, shall be removed from Office on Impeachment for, and Conviction of, Treason, Bribery, or other high Crimes and Misdemeanors.

Article III

SECTION 1.   The judicial Power of the United States, shall be vested in one supreme Court, and in such inferior Courts as the Congress may from time to time ordain and establish. The Judges, both of the supreme and inferior Courts, shall hold their Offices during good Behaviour, and shall, at stated Times, receive for their Services, a Compensation, which shall not be diminished during their Continuance in Office.

SECTION 2.   The judicial Power shall extend to all Cases, in Law and Equity, arising under this Constitution, the Laws of the United States, and Treaties made, or which shall be made, under their Authority;—to all Cases affecting Ambassadors, other public Ministers and Consuls;—to all Cases of admiralty and maritime Jurisdiction;—to Controversies to which the United States shall be a Party;—to Controversies between two or more States;—between a State and Citizens of another State;—between Citizens of different States;—between Citizens of the same State claiming Lands under Grants of different States, and between a State, or the Citizens thereof, and foreign States, Citizens or Subjects.

In all Cases affecting Ambassadors, other public Ministers and Consuls, and those in which a State shall be Party, the supreme Court shall have original Jurisdiction. In all the other Cases before mentioned, the supreme Court shall have appellate Jurisdiction, both as to Law and Fact, with such Exceptions, and under such Regulations as the Congress shall make.

The Trial of all Crimes, except in Cases of Impeachment, shall be by Jury; and such Trial shall be held in the State where the said Crimes shall have been committed; but when not committed within any State, the Trial shall be at such Place or Places as the Congress may by Law have directed.

SECTION 3. Treason against the United States, shall consist only in levying War against them, or in adhering to their Enemies, giving them Aid and Comfort. No Person shall be convicted of Treason unless on the Testimony of two Witnesses to the same overt Act, or on Confession in open Court.

The Congress shall have Power to declare the Punishment of Treason, but no Attainder of Treason shall work Corruption of Blood, or Forfeiture except during the Life of the Person attained.

Article IV

SECTION 1. Full Faith and Credit shall be given in each State to the public Acts, Records, and judicial Proceedings of every other State. And the Congress may by general Laws prescribe the Manner in which such Acts, Records and Proceedings shall be proved, and the Effect thereof.

SECTION 2.   The Citizens of each State shall be entitled to all Privileges and Immunities of Citizens in the several States.

A Person charged in any State with Treason, Felony, or other Crime, who shall flee from Justice, and be found in another State, shall on Demand of the executive Authority of the State from which he fled, be delivered up, to be removed to the State having Jurisdiction of the Crime.

No Person held to Service or Labour in one State, under the Laws thereof, escaping into another, shall, in Consequence of any Law or Regulation therein, be discharged from such Service or Labour, but shall be delivered up on Claim of the Party to whom such Service or Labour may be due.

SECTION 3.   New States may be admitted by the Congress into this Union; but no new State shall be formed or erected within the Jurisdiction of any other State; nor any State be formed by the Junction of two or more States, or Parts of States, without the Consent of the Legislatures of the States concerned as well as of the Congress.

The Congress shall have Power to dispose of and make all needful Rules and Regulations respecting the Territory or other Property belonging to the United States; and nothing in this Constitution shall be so construed as to Prejudice any Claims of the United States, or of any particular State.

SECTION 4.   The United States shall guarantee to every State in this Union a Republican Form of Government, and shall protect each of them against Invasion; and on Application of the Legislature, or of the Executive (when the Legislature cannot be convened) against domestic Violence.

Article V

The Congress, whenever two thirds of both Houses shall deem it necessary, shall propose Amendments to this Constitution, or, on the Application of the Legislatures of two thirds of the several States, shall call a Convention for proposing Amendments, which, in either Case, shall be valid to all Intents and Purposes, as Part of this Constitution, when ratified by the Legislatures of three fourths of the several States, or by Conventions in three fourths thereof, as the one or the other Mode of Ratification may be proposed by the Congress; provided that no Amendment which may be made prior to the Year One thousand eight hundred and eight shall in any Manner affect the first and fourth Clauses in the Ninth Section of the first Article; and that no State, without its Consent, shall be deprived of its equal Suffrage in the Senate.

Article VI

All Debts contracted and Engagements entered into, before the Adoption of this Constitution, shall be as valid against the United States under this Constitution, as under the Confederation.

This Constitution, and the Laws of the United States which shall be made in Pursuance thereof; and all Treaties made, or which shall be made, under the Authority of the United States, shall be the supreme Law of the Land; and the Judges in every State shall be bound thereby, any Thing in the Constitution or Laws of any State to the Contrary notwithstanding.

The Senators and Representatives before mentioned, and the Members of the several State Legislatures, and all executive and judicial Officers, both of the United States and of the several States, shall be bound by Oath or Affirmation, to support this Constitution; but no religious Test shall ever be required as a Qualification to any Office or public Trust under the United States.

Article VII

The Ratification of the Conventions of nine States, shall be sufficient for the Establishment of this Constitution between the States so ratifying the Same.

ARTICLES IN ADDITION TO, AND AMENDMENT OF, THE CONSTITUTION OF THE UNITED STATES OF AMERICA, PROPOSED BY CONGRESS, AND RATIFIED BY THE LEGISLATURES OF THE SEVERAL STATES, PURSUANT TO THE FIFTH ARTICLE OF THE ORIGINAL CONSTITUTION.

Amendment I [1791]

Congress shall make no law respecting an establishment of religion, or prohibiting the free exercise thereof; or abridging the freedom of speech, or of the press; or the right of the people peaceably to assemble, and to petition the Government for a redress of grievances.

Amendment II [1791]

A well regulated Militia, being necessary to the security of a free State, the right of the people to keep and bear Arms, shall not be infringed.

Amendment III [1791]

No Soldier shall, in time of peace be quartered in any house, without the consent of the Owner, nor in time of war, but in a manner to be prescribed by law.

Amendment IV [1791]

The right of the people to be secure in their persons, houses, papers, and effects, against unreasonable searches and seizures, shall not be violated, and no Warrants shall issue, but upon probable cause, supported by Oath or affirmation, and particularly describing the place to be searched, and the persons or things to be seized.

Amendment V [1791]

No person shall be held to answer for a capital, or otherwise infamous crime, unless on a presentment or indictment of a Grand Jury, except in cases arising in the land or naval forces, or in the Militia, when in actual service in time of War or public danger; nor shall any person be subject for the same offence to be twice put in jeopardy of life or limb; nor shall be compelled in any criminal case to be a witness against himself, nor be deprived of life, liberty, or property, without due process of law; nor shall private property be taken for public use, without just compensation.

Amendment VI [1791]

In all criminal prosecutions, the accused shall enjoy the right to a speedy and public trial, by an impartial jury of the State and district wherein the crime shall have been committed, which district shall have been previously ascertained by law, and to be informed of the nature and cause of the accusation; to be confronted with the Witnesses against him; to have compulsory process for obtaining witnesses in his favor, and to have the Assistance of Counsel for his defence.

Amendment VII [1791]

In Suits at common law, where the value in controversy shall exceed twenty dollars, the right of trial by jury shall be preserved, and no fact tried by a jury, shall be otherwise re-examined in any Court of the United States, than according to the rules of the common law.

Amendment VIII [1791]

Excessive bail shall not be required, nor excessive fines imposed, nor cruel and unusual punishments inflicted.

Amendment IX [1791]

The enumeration in the Constitution, of certain rights, shall not be construed to deny or disparage others retained by the people.

Amendment X [1791]

The powers not delegated to the United States by the Constitution, nor prohibited by it to the States, are reserved to the States respectively, or to the people.

Amendment XI [1798]

The Judicial power of the United States shall not be construed to extend to any suit in law or equity, commenced or prosecuted against one of the United States by Citizens of another State, or by Citizens or Subjects of any Foreign State.

Amendment XII [1804]

The Electors shall meet in their respective states and vote by ballot for President and Vice-President, one of whom, at least, shall not be an inhabitant of the same state with themselves; they shall name in their ballots the person voted for as President, and in distinct ballots the person voted for as Vice-President, and they shall make distinct lists of all persons voted for as President, and of all persons voted for as Vice-President, and of the number of votes for each, which lists they shall sign and certify, and transmit sealed to the seat of the government of the United States, directed to the President of the Senate;— The President of the Senate shall, in the presence of the Senate and House of Representatives, open all the certificates and the votes shall then be counted;—The person having the greatest number of votes for President, shall be the President, if such number be a majority of the whole number of Electors appointed; and if no person have such majority, then from the persons having the highest numbers not exceeding three on the list of those voted for as President, the House of Representatives shall choose immediately, by ballot, the President. But in choosing the President, the votes shall be taken by states, the representation from each state having one vote; a quorum for this purpose shall consist of a member or members from two-thirds of the states, and a majority of all the states shall be necessary to a choice. And if the House of Representatives shall not choose a President whenever the right of choice shall devolve upon them, before the fourth day of March next following, then the Vice-President shall act as President, as in the case of the death or other constitutional disability of the President. The person having the greatest number of votes as Vice-President, shall be the Vice-President, if such number be a majority of the whole number of Electors appointed, and if no person have a majority, then from the two highest numbers on the list, the Senate shall choose the Vice-President; a quorum for the purpose shall consist of two-thirds of the whole number of Senators, and a majority of the whole number shall be necessary to a choice. But no person constitutionally ineligible to the office of President shall be eligible to that of Vice-President of the United States.

Amendment XIII [1865]

SECTION 1.   Neither slavery nor involuntary servitude, except as a punishment for crime whereof the party shall have been duly convicted, shall exist within the United States, or any place subject to their jurisdiction.

SECTION 2.   Congress shall have power to enforce this article by appropriate legislation.

Amendment XIV [1868]

SECTION 1.   All persons born or naturalized in the United States, and subject to the jurisdiction thereof, are citizens of the United States and of the State wherein they reside. No State shall make or enforce any law which shall abridge the privileges or immunities of citizens of the United States; nor shall any State deprive any person of life, liberty, or property, without due process of law; nor deny to any person within its jurisdiction the equal protection of the laws.

SECTION 2.   Representatives shall be apportioned among the several States according to their respective numbers, counting the whole number of persons in each State, excluding Indians not taxed. But when the right to vote at any election for the choice of electors for President and Vice President of the United States, Representatives in Congress, the Executive and Judicial officers of a State, or the members of the Legislature thereof, is denied to any of the male inhabitants of such State, being twenty-one years of age, and citizens of the United States, or in any way abridged, except for participation in rebellion, or other crime, the basis of representation therein shall be reduced in the proportion which the number of such male citizens shall bear to the whole number of male citizens twenty-one years of age in such State.

SECTION 3.   No person shall be a Senator or Representative in Congress, or elector of President and Vice President, or hold any office, civil or military, under the United States, or under any State, who, having previously taken an oath, as a member of Congress, or as an officer of the United States, or as a member of any State legislature, or as an executive or judicial officer of any State, to support the Constitution of the United States, shall have engaged in insurrection or rebellion against the same, or given aid or comfort to the enemies thereof. But Congress may by a vote of two-thirds of each House, remove such disability.

SECTION 4.   The validity of the public debt of the United States, authorized by law, including debts incurred for payment of pensions and bounties for services in suppressing insurrection or rebellion, shall not be questioned. But neither the United States nor any State shall assume or pay any debt or obligation incurred in aid of insurrection or rebellion against the United States, or any claim for the loss or emancipation of any slave; but all such debts, obligations and claims shall be held illegal and void.

SECTION 5.   The Congress shall have power to enforce, by appropriate legislation, the provisions of this article.

Amendment XV [1870]

SECTION 1.   The right of citizens of the United States to vote shall not be denied or abridged by the United States or by any State on account of race, color, or previous condition of servitude.

SECTION 2.   The Congress shall have power to enforce this article by appropriate legislation.

Amendment XVI [1913]

The Congress shall have power to lay and collect taxes on incomes, from whatever source derived, without apportionment among the several States, and without regard to any census or enumeration.

Amendment XVII [1913]

The Senate of the United States shall be composed of two Senators from each State, elected by the people thereof, for six years; and each Senator shall have one vote. The electors in each State shall have the qualifications requisite for electors of the most numerous branch of the State legislatures.

When vacancies happen in the representation of any State in the Senate, the executive authority of such State shall issue writs of election to fill such vacancies: *Provided,* That the legislature of any State may empower the executive thereof to make temporary appointments until the people fill the vacancies by election as the legislature may direct.

This amendment shall not be so construed as to affect the election or term of any Senator chosen before it becomes valid as part of the Constitution.

Amendment XVIII [1919]

SECTION 1. After one year from the ratification of this article the manufacture, sale, or transportation of intoxicating liquors within, the importation thereof into, or the exportation thereof from the United States and all territory subject to the jurisdiction thereof for beverage purposes is hereby prohibited.

SECTION 2. The Congress and the several States shall have concurrent power to enforce this article by appropriate legislation.

SECTION 3. This article shall be inoperative unless it shall have been ratified as an amendment to the Constitution by the legislatures of the several States, as provided in the Constitution, within seven years from the date of the submission hereof to the States by the Congress.

Amendment XIX [1920]

The right of citizens of the United States to vote shall not be denied or abridged by the United States or by any State on account of sex.

Amendment XX [1933]

SECTION 1.   The terms of the President and Vice President shall end at noon on the 20th day of January, and the terms of Senators and Representatives at noon on the 3d day of January, of the years in which such terms would have ended if this article had not been ratified; and the terms of their successors shall then begin.

SECTION 2.   The Congress shall assemble at least once in every year, and such meeting shall begin at noon on the 3d day of January, unless they shall by law appoint a different day.

SECTION 3.   If, at the time fixed for the beginning of the term of the President, the President elect shall have died, the Vice President elect shall become President. If a President shall not have been chosen before the time fixed for the beginning of his term, or if the President elect shall have failed to qualify, then the Vice President elect shall act as President until a President shall have qualified; and the Congress may by law provide for the case wherein neither a President elect nor a Vice President elect shall have qualified, declaring who shall then act as President, or the manner in which one who is to act shall be selected, and such person shall act accordingly until a President or Vice President shall have qualified.

SECTION 4.   The Congress may by law provide for the case of the death of any of the persons from whom the House of Representatives may choose a President whenever the right of choice shall have devolved upon them, and for the case of the death of any of the persons from whom the Senate may choose a Vice President whenever the right of choice shall have devolved upon them.

SECTION 5.   Sections 1 and 2 shall take effect on the 15th day of October following the ratification of this article.

SECTION 6.   This article shall be inoperative unless it shall have been ratified as an amendment to the Constitution by the legislatures of three-fourths of the several States within seven years from the date of its submission.

Amendment XXI [1933]

SECTION 1.   The eighteenth article of amendment to the Constitution of the United States is hereby repealed.

SECTION 2.   The transportation or importation into any State, Territory, or possession of the United States for delivery or use therein of intoxicating liquors, in violation of the laws thereof, is hereby prohibited.

SECTION 3.   This article shall be inoperative unless it shall have been ratified as an amendment to the Constitution by conventions in the several States, as provided in the Constitution, within seven years from the date of the submission hereof to the States by the Congress.

Amendment XXII [1951]

SECTION 1.   No person shall be elected to the office of the President more than twice, and no person who has held the office of President, or acted as President, for more than two years of a term to which some other person was elected President shall be elected to the office of the President more than once. But this Article shall not apply to any person holding the office of President when this Article was proposed by the Congress, and shall not prevent any person who may be holding the office of President, or acting as President, during the term within which this Article becomes operative from holding the office of President or acting as President during the remainder of such term.

SECTION 2.   This article shall be inoperative unless it shall have been ratified as an amendment to the Constitution by the legislatures of three-fourths of the several States within seven years from the date of its submission to the States by the Congress.

Amendment XXIII [1961]

SECTION 1.   The District constituting the seat of Government of the United States shall appoint in such manner as the Congress may direct:

A number of electors of President and Vice President equal to the whole number of Senators and Representatives in Congress to which the District would be entitled if it were a State, but in no event more than the least populous State; they shall be in addition to those appointed by the States, but they shall be considered, for the purposes of the election of President and

Vice President, to be electors appointed by a State; and they shall meet in the District and perform such duties as provided by the twelfth article of amendment.

SECTION 2. The Congress shall have power to enforce this article by appropriate legislation.

Amendment XXIV [1964]

SECTION 1. The right of citizens of the United States to vote in any primary or other election for President or Vice President, for electors for President or Vice President, or for Senator or Representative in Congress, shall not be denied or abridged by the United States or any State by reason of failure to pay any poll tax or other tax.

SECTION 2. The Congress shall have power to enforce this article by appropriate legislation.

Amendment XXV [1967]

SECTION 1. In case of the removal of the President from office or of his death or resignation, the Vice President shall become President.

SECTION 2. Whenever there is a vacancy in the office of the Vice President, the President shall nominate a Vice President who shall take office upon confirmation by a majority vote of both Houses of Congress.

SECTION 3. Whenever the President transmits to the President pro tempore of the Senate and the Speaker of the House of Representatives his written declaration that he is unable to discharge the powers and duties of his office, and until he transmits to them a written declaration to the contrary, such powers and duties shall be discharged by the Vice President as Acting President.

SECTION 4.   Whenever the Vice President and a majority of either the principal officers of the executive departments or of such other body as Congress may by law provide, transmit to the President pro tempore of the Senate and the Speaker of the House of Representatives their written declaration that the President is unable to discharge the powers and duties of his office, the Vice President shall immediately assume the powers and duties of the office as Acting President.

Thereafter, when the President transmits to the President pro tempore of the Senate and the Speaker of the House of Representatives his written declaration that no inability exists, he shall resume the powers and duties of his office unless the Vice President and a majority of either the principal officers of the executive department or of such other body as Congress may by law provide, transmit within four days to the President pro tempore of the Senate and the Speaker of the House of Representatives their written declaration that the President is unable to discharge the powers and duties of his office. Thereupon Congress shall decide the issue, assembling within forty-eight hours for that purpose if not in session. If the Congress, within twenty-one days after receipt of the latter written declaration, or, if Congress is not in session, within twenty-one days after Congress is required to assemble, determines by two-thirds vote of both Houses that the President is unable to discharge the powers and duties of his office, the Vice President shall continue to discharge the same as Acting President; otherwise, the President shall resume the powers and duties of his office.

Amendment XXVI [1971]

SECTION 1.   The right of citizens of the United States, who are eighteen years of age or older, to vote shall not be denied or abridged by the United States or by any State on account of age.

SECTION 2.   The Congress shall have power to enforce this article by appropriate legislation.

BIBLIOGRAPHY

Background

There are many books about the period from before the Revolution to the election of Washington; the books listed here are both well written and scholarly.

Middlekauff, Robert. *The Glorious Cause: The American Revolution 1763–1789.* New York: Oxford University Press, 1982.

Morison, Samuel Eliot, and Commager, Henry Steele. *The Growth of the American Republic.* Vol. 1. New York: Oxford University Press, 1962.

The Constitutional Convention

These books discuss the events at the Constitutional Convention in general, without emphasis on one particular individual or issue.

Bowen, Catherine Drinker. *Miracle at Philadelphia.* Boston: Little, Brown & Co., 1966.

Farrand, Max. *The Framing of the Constitution of the United States of America.* New Haven: Yale University Press, 1913.

Farrand, Max. *The Fathers of the Constitution.* New Haven: Yale University Press, 1921.

Morris, Richard. *Framing of the Federal Constitution.* Washington, D.C.: Government Printing Office, 1979.

Van Doren, Carl. *The Great Rehearsal.* New York: Viking Press, 1948.

Wills, Garry. *Explaining America: the Federalist.* New York: Penguin Books, 1981.

Biographies

The following books include biographies of people highlighted in this book as well as biographies of some other people who played important roles at the Convention.

Ammon, Harry. *James Monroe: The Quest for National Identity.* New York: Norton, 1971.

Clark, Ronald. *Benjamin Franklin: A Biography.* New York: Random House, 1983.

Flexner, James Thomas. *Washington: The Indispensable Man.* Boston: Little, Brown & Co., 1969.

Franklin, Benjamin. *The Autobiography of Benjamin Franklin.* New York: Macmillan, 1962.

Malone, Dumas. *Jefferson and His Time,* 5 vols. Boston: Little, Brown & Co., 1948–75.

O'Connor, John E., *William Paterson: Lawyer and Statesman.* New Brunswick, N.J.: Rutgers University Press, 1979.

Reardon, John J. *Edmund Randolph.* New York: Macmillan, Inc., 1974.

Rutland, R. A. *George Mason: Reluctant Statesman.* Charlottesville: University Press of Virginia, 1961.

Smith, Charles Page. *James Wilson, Founding Father.* Chapel Hill: University of North Carolina Press, 1956.

Stourzh, Gerald. *Alexander Hamilton and the Idea of Republican Government.* Stanford: Stanford University Press, 1970.

Special Works

The first two books are the most important ones written about the Constitution. No one can truly understand the Convention or the Constitution without a study of these books. The Farrand book is the basic source for almost everything that has ever been written about the Constitutional Convention. It brings together in one place the notes of Madison, the official records of the Convention, and many letters from people who participated in the Convention. It is one of the great works of American history and it is out of print. The Mentor edition of *The Federalist Papers* has been used by hundreds of thousands of students. It has two special features. It has a short, but very useful introduction, and it has a copy of the Constitution at the end with references to pages in the *Federalist* that discuss that portion of the document.

The Federalist Papers. New York: Mentor Books, 1961.

Farrand, Max. *Records of the Federal Convention of 1787.* New Haven: Yale University Press, 1937.

The next two books are important because they present both sides of a debate that raged for fifty years: does the Constitution represent only the narrow views of a small group of people who wanted to protect their own economic interests, or was it a document for all people?

Beard, Charles A. *An Economic Interpretation of the Constitution.* 1913.

Brown, Robert E. *Charles Beard and the Constitution.* 1956.

I N D E X